SOUL MUSIC BLACK & WHITE

Johannes Riedel

The Influence of Black Music on the Churches

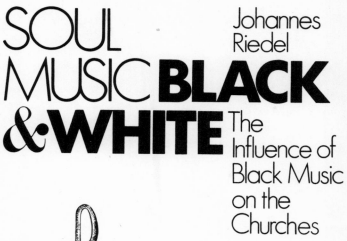

Augsburg Publishing House
Minneapolis, Minnesota

SOUL MUSIC: BLACK AND WHITE

Copyright © 1975 Augsburg Publishing House

Library of Congress Catalog Card No. 73-88611

International Standard Book No. 0-8066-1414-5

Scripture quotations unless otherwise noted are from the Revised
Standard Version of the Bible, copyright 1946, 1952, and 1971 by
the Division of Christian Education of the National Council of
Churches.

Manufactured in the United States of America.

To Adalberto Ortiz
Author of *Yuyungo*

Historia de un negro, una isla y otros negros

ACKNOWLEDGEMENTS

The author wishes to thank the copyright holders for permission to quote excerpts from the following:

"The ballad of holy history" copyright 1966 by John Schultz.

"Jesus was just a good guy" © copyright 1969 by Sacred Songs (A Division of Word, Inc.) in *More Folk Songs for Young Folk.* All rights reserved. Used by permission.

"Christ is changing everything" by Norman Habel, from *For Mature Adults Only,* copyright 1969 by Fortress Press.

"Who's that guy?" copyright 1970 by Richard K. Avery and Donald S. Marsh from *More, More More.* Used by permission of Proclamation Productions, Inc. Orange Square, Port Jervis, N.Y. 12771.

"All the world's a seeker" used by permission from *Songs to Be Sung,* edited by J. Lorne Peachey, copyright 1969 by Herald Press, Scottdale, Pa. 15683 and Faith and Life Press, Newton, Kansas 67114.

"Shared bread" © copyright by Summerlin Music Co.

"O give me a soapbox" © copyright 1971 by Singspiration, Inc. All rights reserved. Used by permission.

"I heard about" by Ralph Carmichael. © copyright 1957 by Lexicon Music, Inc. All rights reserved. International copyright secured. Used by special permission. Performance rights licensed through ASCAP.

"He's listening" by Flo Price, © copyright 1969 by Lexicon Music, Inc. All rights reserved. International copyright secured. Used by special permission. Performance rights licensed through ASCAP.

The quotes from "Clap your hands" and "Run, come see" have been reprinted with permission of the copyright owner, F. E. L. Publications, Ltd. 1925 Pontius Ave., Los Angeles, CA 90025. Phone: (213) 478-0053. Further reproduction is not permitted without written permission of the copyright owner.

Contents

Preface 7

1. Why Black Music and Church Music? 9

2. African Origin of Black Music 19

3. Black Music Comes to the New World 33

4. "Soul" Music of the Black Community 47

5. "Soul" Music Qualities in European-
   American Culture 63

6. American Popular Music and the Blacks 81

7. Folk, Jazz, Pop, and Rock Masses 91

8. The New Folk Hymn 109

9. Criteria for Evaluating New Church Music .. 121

10. The Future of Church Music in America 137

    Notes 149

    Appendix 157

    A Short List of Additional Readings

    A Short List of Recordings

Preface

Perhaps the most distinctive feature of this book is its pan-American perspective. For 10 years I lived in Ecuador, South America. As a musician, church musician, and artistic director for the largest Ecuadorean record company in Guayaquil, Ecuador, I came to know and love the sound and soul of American and Latin American popular music.

My pan-American perspective enlarged as I went on to live and work in North America. Teaching interdisciplinary courses on American music, American popular music, and the music of Charles Ives in connection with the distinguished American Studies Program of the University of Minnesota, and teaching many church music courses and courses on Latin American music for the Music Department of this same university provided opportunity to continue my research. I am grateful to the University and especially to the hundreds of undergraduate and graduate students who were a continuing source of information and motivation, a constant challenge to animate further inquiry, better presentation, and documentation.

Many persons have helped me to give shape and contents to this work. A word of recognition must be given to the composers Bruce Prince-Joseph, Ed Summerlin, and Frank Tirro, who made some of their scores available. Many others gave me access to their valuable tapes and scores. Of my student friends I must give thanks to Nina Archabal for her positive criticism; to Paul Kaatrud for his contributions to the information on American Popular Music; to all student participants in the workshop on Church Music Black-White (Ives Festival II, 1971); to Bertus F. Polman for important assistance in the early stages of research. Without their timely help, this work would not have been completed.

Why Black Music and Church Music?

To the foreigner, American music means black music, spirituals, jazz, and soul. Many Japanese, Germans, French, Czechs, and Scandinavians listen to this music with rapture. They even enjoy singing their own arrangements of American music. School children in these countries learn black American music. They are told, "This is America." For them, the American musician is black. Are they wrong? Do we think of American music as black music? Is it?

Recognition that black music, black musicians, and black musical styles have exerted an overpowering influence on the sounds and rhythms of white music, sacred and secular, is long overdue. Music for the masses in America, for congregations, for mass, open-air recitals, for millions of radio and TV listeners is music with "the beat," the beat of popular music, of show music, of revival music. But Americans do not realize that this music came from black American music. The drums of Africa, the drums of the honkey-tonks in New Orleans and St. Louis, and the drums of the speakeasies have given their rhythmic pulse to American music.

We can speak of genuine American music only in this century, at a time when black music came to the fore, first, in the art of ragtime, and then in the art of jazz. The sound of ragtime was eternalized in many of the compositions of America's greatest composer, Charles Ives. The sound of jazz permeates many of the works of Aaron Copland. Although many Americans take great pride in the works of these composers, few know that these composers have fallen under the spell of ragtime and jazz. Today we are more aware of the beauty and magnitude of black music, the kind of catharsis it creates in the listener. Only slowly are we coming to appreciate the influential role black musicians have played in the American music of today and of yesterday.

The renewed interest in ragtime music is evidenced in the New York Public Library's two-volume publication of the works of Scott Joplin, the greatest of all ragtime musicians. The black Joplin takes his place beside the white Stephen Foster, whose music owes a heavy debt to black music of the past century, as the only American composers to be honored with complete editions.

The recent death of gospel singer Mahalia Jackson, grandchild of plantation slaves, moved millions of white concert-goers who had heard her sing at Carnegie Hall in New York, at the Berlin *Sportpalast,* or the Frederick Mann Auditorium in Tel Aviv.

What would white pop music have done without the impact of the black gospel sound? Tony Heilbut in his *The Gospel Sound* puts it well:

All rock's most resilient features, the beat, the

drama, the group vibrations derive from gospel. From the rock symphonies to detergent commercials, from Aretha Franklin's prototechnique to the Beatles' harmonies, gospel has simply reformed all our listening expectations. The very tension between beats, the climax we anticipate almost subliminally is straight out of the church. The dance steps that ushered in a new physical freedom were copied from the shout, the holy dance of "victory." The sit-ins soothed by hymns, the freedom marches powered by shouts, the "brother and sister" fraternity of revolution: the gospel church gave us all of these.[1]

Its effect on white young people is electrifying, "a force that can light a room." The power of soul music moves white and black alike. Soul musicians seem to communicate honestly from the deepest recesses of their personalities. The beauty of their expression emanates from the rumble of gospel chords and the plaintive cry of the blues. They combine burning emotional conviction, a strong rhythmic pulse, and earthy lyrics.

The nationwide popularity of black soul music is undeniable. It can be heard on the top 40s, in the suburbs as well as the ghettos, and on midwestern campuses as well as in Harlem's Apollo Theatre. The popularity of soul music is particularly significant for the black population as a badge of identity. As Charles Keil said in his recent book on black music, soul refers to the entire catalog of black culture. For many of today's black Americans, soul is the living expression of black history and culture.

Eileen Southern's most recent books, *The Music of Black Americans* and *Readings in Black American Music,* inform white people about the uninterrupted contribution of black Americans to church, classical, folk,

11

and popular music. She describes the increasing activity of black musicians in the performance of operas and symphonies as singers, instrumentalists, and conductors. Southern's studies provide a wealth of previously unknown information on the black music in the eighteenth century, on the significance of black performers in the nineteenth century, on the great contribution of black composers to classical and popular music in the twentieth century.

The establishment of Afro-American studies departments at many American universities in the 1960s is a hopeful sign. They help blacks and whites alike to know and to take pride in black history and achievements. Many white and black students enroll in Afro-American studies courses. Surveys of the backgrounds of American black music and of the various phases in black music in America are central to most Afro-American studies departments.

The idea that churches deliberately cultivate racist attitudes toward black music is patently absurd. Yet many church authorities are reluctant to correct racist attitudes. The musical standard is set by the traditions of the chorales and gospel songs. However, this traditional standard too often is confused with mere nostalgia for days gone by. The church reflects the general trend toward nostalgia in America today. Nostalgia impeded needed innovations in church music. Even avant-garde white folk or guitar masses or services belong to this type of nostalgic church music. The folksy, simplistic, sometimes rustic sounds of this music are reminiscent of traditional, sweet-sounding American church music such as the nineteenth century Sunday school hymns of William Bradbury. Most folk and guitar masses unconsciously evoke the memory of church music in the past when whites did not worship with blacks.

Resistance to change has made it difficult for the church to communicate with the people. Words such as *justification, sanctification, atonement,* and *witness* are as obscure to most people as *pop, rock, black,* and *soul* music are to many church musicologists.

This lack of adequate communication for the needs of our time and society even affects authors who have attempted to discuss modern music and the church. For example, Eric Routley in his *Twentieth Century Church Music* discussed the significance of pop and church music in four chapters. However, he passed over the interconnection between pop and black music. William Robert Miller in his *The World of Pop Music and Jazz* discussed jazz masses. However, he pointed out their black essence only indirectly.

Until recently, available information about the black spiritual has been quite misleading. In his voluminous writings on the spirituals, George Pullen Jackson incorrectly stressed the dependence of black spirituals on white Protestant sources. In recent years Alan Lomax refuted Jackson's conclusions, pointedly criticizing Jackson's comparisons of printed versions of melodies and texts of black and white spirituals out of context of their performance. Through what he called "cantometric analysis" Lomax showed that the "main tradition of Afro-American song, especially those of the old-time congregational spiritual, are derived from the main African song style model." [2]

White people are generally not aware that there have been parallels in their own church musical history to the current black interest in soul music. Soul music seems to arise most often among religious groups that find themselves outside the limits of contemporary mainstream religious movements. There were a few such movements in Europe and many of them, of European origin, blossomed in America. In seventeenth century Europe, pietistic Lutherans even anticipated the current term "soul music" in their discussions of *Seelenmusik*. The same continent saw the rise of the Jewish Hasidic self-expressive worshiping through the *mitzvah* (soul dance) and *hitlahavut* (enthusiasm). Many of the sects that came to America to escape religious persecution participated in the self-expressive and ecstatic quality of soul music. The ethereal quality of the music of the Ephrata Cloister, the highly ornamented style of hymn singing practiced even today by the Amish, and even the "reprehensible" tendency of early American Puritan congregations to ornament the psalm tunes all participate in the quality of soul music.

The role black music has played in our land remains largely unknown. In his *Music and Some Highly Musical People* (1891), James M. Trotter gave minute details of the activities of some of the most distinguished black concert artists of the time. Among them he mentioned:

> Elizabeth Taylor Greenfield, the famous songstress, often called "The Black Swan"
> The Luca Family, vocalists and instrumentalists
> Henry F. Williams, composer, band instructor
> Justin Holland, the eminent author and arranger
> Thomas J. Bowers, tenor-vocalist; often styled the "American Mario"
> James Greene Bethune, otherwise known as "Blind Tom," the wonderful pianist
> Anna Madah and Emma Hyers, vocalists and pianists
> Frederick Elliot Lewis, pianist, organist, violinist
> Nellie E. Brown, the favorite New Hampshire vocalist
> Samuel E. Jamieson, the brilliant young pianist

Joseph White, the eminent violinist and composer
The Colored American Opera Company
The Jubilee Singers of Fisk University
The Georgia Minstrels [3]

Contemporary classical music written by black composers is now becoming available. The works recorded range from a moderate contemporary style such as that of William Grant Still to the avant-garde musical language of T. J. Anderson. Notable recordings include the *Festive Overture* (CRI SD 259) and *Afro-American Symphony* (Col. M-32782) of William Grant Still, the dean of black composers; Howard Swanson's *Short Symphony* (CRI SD 254); Ulysses Kay's *Serenade for Orchestra* (Louisville 548-8) and *Sinfonia in E* (CRI 139); Julia Perry's *Short Pieces for Orchestra* (CRI-145) and her delightfully sophisticated "test tube musical baby" *Homunculus, C. F.* [Chord of the Fifteenth] *for Ten Percussionists* (CRI SD 258), a very popular work with symphony orchestras all over the land. The *Seven Songs* of Howard Swanson, including his magnificent setting of Langston Hughes' poem, "The Negro Speaks of Rivers," have been recorded (Desto 6422). Swanson's setting of Hughes' words has given us one of the greatest American art songs of all time.

Despite Trotter's histories and the recordings and publication of the works of black composers, most Americans remain uninformed of black contributions to the story of American music. How many know that one of the earliest band directors in this country was a black? In 1819 Frank Johnson distinguished himself as one of the best performers on the bugle and French horn, and earned his band a rating just below that of the Royal Band of London and the Band of the National Guards at Paris. How many know that the first musical comedy in this country (1866) dealt with The *Black*

15

Crook (with an all-white cast), and that one of the first American composers of musical comedy was a black, Will Marion Cook, whose first black musical comedy sketch, *Clorind and the Origin of the Cakewalk,* was a great success? How many know that Louis Moreau Gottschalk, one of America's greatest piano virtuosos and America's first great composer of piano music, was partly black?

Most of us are aware that American black musicians created jazz. Few of us are aware that for the non-American, American music means an embodiment of rhythm, of the beat. Rhythm has decisively shaped the nature of American popular music in the 20th century, the fox trot, the boogie woogie, swing, and rock. Throughout the 19th century Americans had followed European musical fashions, whether it was the French minuet, the French/English contredanse, the Viennese waltz, the Czech polka, or the German schottische. After a century of European domination American popular music assumed the most influential role in the 20th century. Europeans adopted the rhythmic qualities of American popular music in their own way. Through the beat of black music and its application in popular music, America in the 20th century became a world power in popular music for the first time in her history.

The music of black America has had its impact on every facet of American music—church, folk, classical, and especially popular music. Gian Carlo Menotti's "The Saint of Bleeker Street" is a marvelous example of the merger of classical music, in this case Italian opera, and American popular music with the black beat, jazz orchestration, and "soul." Few people can absorb the spiritual stress, psychological impact, and emotional vehemence of the saint's vision and stigmata aria, written in the best tradition of Italian operatic

16

theatricality but with an accompaniment obviously related to black and popular music. The high-tempered and nervy sound of the "heart motive" of Menotti's *The Consul* exploits the blues sound to rouse, to play on human feelings.[4]

This book concerns the nature of black music, how it came to America, and how it developed into a marvelous and multi-faceted art in the new environs. I hope that this story may provide some new understanding of American black music and especially some honest assessment of its impact on white church music over the years. But the story does not end here. It points the way to new love and reconciliation in the living church through the continuing impact of the rich resources of American black music.

2

African Origin
of Black Music

The appreciation of black music is not new. The
names of such great stars as Ray Charles, Ella Fitzgerald, Nat King Cole, and Louis Armstrong were house-
hold words in the 1950s. Long before the rise of American black identity in the '60s black faces had smiled
from plasticized record jackets and from the shiny
silver screens of television tubes in the living rooms
of white Americans. In the popular mind, these great
stars performed music that was the exclusive property
of America. Most people noted a certain "jazzy" quality, a certain rhythmic jump, in much of the music
American blacks performed, yet Americans seemed to
accept this "jazziness" without questioning its origins.
Any roots the music had, were assumed to be American.

The Search for African Roots

Along with the declaration of black identity in America in the '60s came the association of black Americans

19

with black Africa. The new signs of African identity—hairdos, clothing fashions, verbal clichés—all seemed to unsettle the unconscious paternalistic sensibilities of many white Americans. Blacks were no longer content to be just Americans; they had to be Afro-Americans. In fact, the recovery of Afro-American identity in many ways paralleled the search for other ethnic identities in American life.

A hard core of racial thinking in white American attitudes towards black Americans is evident in the common explanation for the success of blacks in music. The notion that blacks have an intuitive or genetic gift of rhythm attributes the significance of black musical success only to racial factors. This approach seems to be uniquely reserved for blacks, but consider the Italian-American and his great love for opera. Many Italian-Americans can hum the tunes from their favorite Verdi operas, many Italian-Americans sing Neapolitan songs, and it seems that every other name on the roster of New York's Metropolitan Opera Company is Italian. Still, most Americans do not identify love for opera as a racial trait. Instead, the explanation points to a long tradition of singing that can be traced back through the history of Italian music. Such popular wisdom, unfortunately, is not applied to the extraordinary rhythm in American black music. Explanations by racial factors overlook rich African traditions and imply that black Americans have no history or tradition.

The musical heritage of American blacks has received recent recognition as part of the larger effort to recognize African roots and to study African and Afro-American history in the same way European and immigration history have been studied. In cultivating a renewed sense of ethnic identity, American blacks have not, however, abandoned their racial identity. They have tried to combine racial and ethnic identity.

Through the development of ethnic identity they hope to add a missing dimension of historicism from their lives—to humanize themselves in the eyes of other Americans in their own eyes. Such protagonists of the new Afro-American identity as LeRoi Jones and Charles Keil have justly shunned the standard racist explanations that attribute human creativity to irrational instinct.

Along with the proud sense of Afro-American identity, new understandings of American black music based on an accurate picture of the history of blacks in Africa and in America have developed. Jones, for example, in his *Blues People* emphasizes the social history of blacks in American society as an important factor in the development of the blues.

The birth of Afro-American consciousness has not, however, completely eliminated the pattern of racial explanations even on the part of those who have suffered most from them. Ironically, some black Americans have successfully turned the tables and exploited racial stereotypes to their own advantage. They have promoted the belief that American black music and musicians have "soul" and that soul is the exclusive property of blacks. Although its meaning is difficult to pinpoint (one black writer has called it an "unspeakable essence"), soul seems generally to refer to a highly desirable innate quality, a quality of almost superhuman capacity for feeling. Whites covet soul, and some blacks as well as some whites unwittingly use soul to promote the notion of black racial superiority.

In the opinion of LeRoi Jones, as a verbal symbol the term "soul" suffers from the absence of any universal denotative function. Yet the very vagueness Jones notes may constitute its main utility. As an indefinable quality, soul cannot be consciously cultivated. Undeniably, soul has served to some extent in bringing about a new and positive image for American blacks.

African Rhythmic Patterns

As part of the exciting exploration of Afro-American history and culture, several theories of African origin are replacing the common assumption that American black music results from the instinctive "jazziness" of black people. J. C. Waterman is one who traces the vitality of American black music to its African roots. He believes that the jazziness of American black music is an outgrowth of a metronomic sense which is essential to both the performance and appreciation of African music. This metronomic sense enables performer and listener to feel a strong regular pulse even while the performer elaborates complex rhythmic patterns.[1] The regularity of the basic pulse of African music seems to invite infinite rhythmic variations around it, and African musicians vigorously and magnificently exploit the possibilities. The variation around the basic pulse involves the alternation, not necessarily regular, of patterns made up of two and of three pulses.

Although the African musical tradition is exceptionally rich in such rhythmic subtlety, the principle is also evident in the history of western music. Moreover, the principle is easier to study as it occurs in western music because of its comparatively limited and simplistic application. The melodies of many Lutheran chorales, for example, illustrate the principle of alternating rhythmic patterns of 3 and 2 pulses while maintaining a constant pulse value, a musical principle known as *hemiola*. Consider, for example, the following phrase from Johann Crüger's well-loved communion hymn "Schmücke dich." [2]

In the sixth measure the pattern of six quarter note pulses falls into two basic beats made up of three quarters as follows:

In the seventh measure, however, the pattern of six quarter note pulses falls into three basic beats made up of two quarters as follows:

The quarter note pulse remains fixed in value throughout the two measures, but an overall effect of rhythmic fluidity is created by grouping the pulses alternately into large patterns of two and three pulses.

The effect of rhythm fluidity depends on the establishment and maintenance of an unflagging pulse. The variation of two-three patterns may occur in any measure which has at least five pulses. Once a regular pulse or *tactus* was established for western music in the 15th century, western European composers almost immediately began to experiment with various groupings of the pulses. Once the steady musical pulse had been established, a fertile musical imagination apparently could not resist the temptation to undermine subtly its regularizing effect.

The music of Central Africa exploits the *hemiola* device extensively. In *Music of Central Africa,* Rose

Brandel suggests that Renaissance man, accustomed as he was to the incessant subtle alternation of pulse groupings, might feel more secure than we do with the rhythmic subtleties of Central African music. We are heirs to the musical legacy of the 18th and 19th centuries, when European composers cast their music into relatively regular rhythmic patterns as if to stabilize one facet of music in order to allow for explorations in other areas such as harmony, sonority, and form. But these explorations came at the cost of greatly reduced rhythmic vitality. Only in the 20th century have composers working within the mainstream of the western musical tradition shown renewed interest in irregular rhythms. Their interest in some part may reflect the historical revival of Renaissance music as well as interest in the music of Central Africa, both in its indigenous form and in its development by Afro-American musicians.

The regular pulse of African music lends itself not only to various linear groupings such as we saw in the hymn example above, but also to various vertical groupings which occur when several parts, voices, or instruments sing or play different rhythmic patterns of two and three pulses at the same time. Consider again a basic six-pulse phrase. One player may pattern the pulses into two groups of three pulses while a second player patterns the pulses into three groups of two pulses. The following examples from the work of the 17th century composer Heinrich Schütz illustrates the principle of vertical hemiola or cross rhythm.[3]

In this case the effect of fluidity depends on the various parts each having their own pattern of alternating two-three pulse groupings. The Schütz example, however, illustrates the principle of cross rhythm at a relatively simple level. Consider, for example, one drum playing a pattern of 7 pulses by alternating groups of twos and threes along with three or four other players with their own individualized rhythmic designs. Some possible rhythmic variations within a phrase of seven pulses articulated by three independent voices might be:

In African music such cross rhythms are often played by drums or other percussion instruments. With the musical imagination focused mainly on rhythm, the variety available through linear and vertical hemiola is endless. Along with the flexible rhythmic patterning, there are other dimensions of subtlety available through combining percussion instruments of various sounds (timbres) and combining human voices and instruments.

African Musical Instruments

The instruments through which the rhythmic subtlety of African music is expressed are largely of the percussion type. The African environment is an unusually good provider of materials suitable for making instruments: trees, animal skins, horns, and gourds, to mention only the most obvious ones. The Bantus of Central Africa possess a rich folk literature that tells much about the "origins" of their instruments and music. This literature tells of a certain Marimba, a beautiful chieftainess of the Wakanbi tribe who gave the Bantu their oldest and most beautiful songs and who invented many musical instruments for them. Marimba allegedly guided the Bantu in the creation of the xylophone, called *marimba* after the lovely chieftainess, and invented the drum from an old mortar bowl which the village women had worn through to the bottom. Credo Mutwa describes the event: "for the first time since the dawn of creation, the forests shook to the pulsing beat."

The drums seem to touch every facet of African life. From the beginning, the drums held a place in African religious ceremony.

> The largest drums she [Marimba] ordered to be reserved for purposes of worship only, and these had the symbol of the River of Eternity carved into them in a continuous pattern all round, and on many of these drums were also carved symbols representing passages from the great poems of creation and sacred symbols of spiritual secret knowledge. This she did to preserve the knowledge of the Wakambi for all time.[4]

The drum also, however, played a vital part in the routine aspects of African life. The "talking drums" of Africa accompany every phase of village life. These drums enable the African villager to penetrate his environment and to communicate over stretches of difficult terrain. They carry the messages of everyday life; they are the telephones of primitive village life. Many of the messages heard through the day and night convey information of no great importance. A man's drum signal may simply mean that he will be late getting back from the day's business, or it may tell of the birth of a child to a father who is away from home. The drums "talk" through linear patterns which alternate high- and low-pitched sounds.

African languages, like the Chinese language, utilize pitch differentiation; that is, the same combination of syllables may have different meanings when uttered on different pitches. By comparison, the effect of changes of pitch on the meanings of English words is negligible. In the African languages, each syllable may be spoken in either a high or low tone. Thus, there are four ways to accent a two-syllable word. Consider the Bantu word *longo*. When both syllables are uttered in low tones, the meaning is *irritation;* when both are uttered in high tones, there is no meaning; when the first is high, and the second low, the meaning is *hill,* and when the first is low, and the second high, the meaning is *skull.*

Drum language borrows the alternation of high and low tones from the spoken African languages. Obviously, the drums cannot articulate specific syllables such as *lon* or *go.* To circumvent this limitation, the drummer substitutes the pitch patterns of a given repertory of traditional sayings and proverbs for the syllables of specific words. For example, in sending a message announcing the birth of a child, the drummer would play the pattern of high and low pitches for the well-known saying: "Set the heart down, the child has not set down his feet in the black body of the mother." [5]

Although African music has an extraordinary wealth of percussion instruments that speak incredibly complex and subtle rhythms, many of these same instruments also speak qualities of melody and harmony and participate in marvelous effects of tone color and even orchestration. Along with some percussion instruments such as the marimba, many stringed and wind instru-

27

ments such as lyres, harps, thumb pianos, and even the human voice exploit these musical qualities.

African Singing

Most African melodies tend to descend slowly through the entire range of the melody. The following melody heard in former French Equatorial Africa, a Bongili girl's banana work song, drops down a sheer octave without any stops or detours.[6]

The use of harmony is prevalent throughout Africa, although some groups such as the Dahomeans use almost no harmony at all, while others such as the Ashanti apply at least two-part and frequently three- and four-part harmony in almost all of their music. African harmony typically involves parallel motion by intervals or chord progressions. An Okandi women's dance song from former French Equatorial Africa illustrates the parallelism in African harmony.[7]

African singers tend to sing with an emphatic and full voice and without any vibrato. Most men sing in the highest ranges of their voices, and vocal timbres are often tense, hoarse, and somewhat gutteral. Singers create special vocal effects by shouting, glissando, excessive nasality, yodeling, humming, and by imitating a variety of animal sounds.

Favorite among African song forms is a litany-like structure often combined with a call-response performance pattern. These litany-like structures usually involve enumerations and supplications directed to a deity. A leader pronounces these supplications while the assembly of the faithful repeats over and over again the same or approximately the same insistent cries for divine help and assistance. In the singing of these repetitive litany-like pieces, the participants have a musical experience similar to the experience of rock music with its endless repetitions of ostinato or ground bass patterns. The singing of the repetitive African litanies may provoke a communal mood, a communal group arousal of almost hypnotic dimensions. The minds of the litanists become oblivious to the world around them to the extent that they may sense a direct response from the deity. They may also sense alleviation and resolution similar to that experienced by the American black prisoners at the State Prison Farm at Jennings, Louisiana, who sing a litany (see Chapter 4) to escape their threat-laden life in a southern prison.

The sacrificial ceremonies of the African Tohoussu provide beautiful examples of ritualistic litanies. The ceremonies of this cult take place over a period of four days and involve twenty designated temples. The liturgy of the sacrifice of the bull consists of twelve ritual litanies in which call and response performance patterns play a major role. In the funeral song within this liturgy, the soloist sings twenty-three litany supplications which are repeated literally by a women's chorus of litanists.

African Orchestration

These Tohoussu sacrificial ceremonies also reveal black Africa's marvelous wisdom and knowledge about orchestration.[8] The anonymous composers of the Tohoussu liturgy of the sacrifice of the bull have carefully planned the distribution of vocal and instrumental pieces and pieces which combine vocal and instrumental forces. In only the processional and recessional do instrumentalists perform with the vocal parts. In Nos. 5 and 8 only the instruments play; No. 3 consists of a vocal solo; and No. 9 contains a solo-choral section. In all other sections complete vocal or instrumental ensembles prevail. The specific location and contrast of the vocal and instrumental numbers is essential in this institutionalized service, a service which flows from and to a few-voiced ensemble, proceeding through various many-voiced numbers, some for chorus, some for solo and chorus, and others for various instruments. The instruments are introduced in various ways. Sometimes they appear in a terraced configuration, one following immediately upon the other; other times, one instrument is used for one section, another instrument for another section; sometimes all instruments are introduced at the same time.

Music, Religion, and Life

Thus, from the ordinary messages of the incessantly talking drums to the sacred sacrificial cults, music permeates every aspect of life in black Africa. Life is music for the black man in Africa, and music is also life. Life is religion for him. Life, music and religion are one and inseparable. Religion is not merely a side of life; music is not merely a side of life. Religion is *the way* life is lived, socialized, formalized in ritual by means of music and dance. Most of life's activities fall within the total magic religious scheme, and most of the musical activities fall within the religion-life complex. Through his rituals, mythologies, and musical representation, the black African expresses his great concern and involvement with his deities. He strongly interacts with these deities through his various liturgical ceremonies and their associated music. He has thereby sought harmony with the deities in matters of life—involving himself, his fellow men, plants and animals—and even in death. To the African, every aspect of life participates in an integral *one* which gives meaning to all of existence. Life, religion, and music all belong to the *magnum opus dei*.

3

Black Music
Comes to the New World

Transfer of music from one continent to another, from one country to another, has been central to the development of American music. Two basic transfers have influenced American church music: the transfer of Calvinistic/Puritan, French/English music and of African music. Both gave shape and nature to American church music. They have many things in common, but there are also some remarkable differences. While the transfer of Puritan music was a voluntary one accompanying the pilgrims to a new Eden, the transfer of African music was a forced one accompanying blacks to a foreign land, to the hell of slavery. While the transfer of Puritan music occurred in a smooth, almost imperceptible fashion soaking the entire corpus of American church music with its concept of music-making and the church, the transfer of African music occurred in a less smooth fashion. However, once it had found its own Afro-American expression in the form of the spiritual, blues, and gospel songs, it left its mark on American church music in the form of its concepts of rhythm and beat.

Despite the clear differences in origin and in the transfer process, there are some notable similarities between the Calvinist/Puritan and Afro-American churches and their music. In both the Calvinist/Puritan and Afro-American churches lay members participated in the musical realization of the worship service through the leader and the congregation sharing in the responsive singing of psalms and spiritual songs. In both churches rote singing predominated over singing by note. In both churches improvisation was cultivated.[1] In both churches there was little place for truly classical church music and neither church was very receptive to great classical instrumental (organ) music.

A second movement of church music from England to America occurred in the transfer of 18th century English revivalism and its music. The revivalistic music preceded by the texts of Isaac Watts, and the revivalistic music of the Wesleys, and Afro-American music, also have various things in common.

Thus the transfer of African music to the Americas is just one chapter in the history of various transfers of church music from the other side of the Atlantic to this country. It is, however, the most significant and surely the most exciting one. The initial phase of this transfer involved the gradual merging of Euro-American and African musical concepts to yield the Afro-American spiritual.

When the Negro slave was brought to America, he naturally sang the songs he had sung in Africa—work songs and shouts filled with religious appeals and praises. His many deities were personal gods who were out in the fields with him, at home with him, who attended his celebrations and ceremonies. These songs were probably performed responsively in a call-and-response pattern between a leader and a group. The phrases and the songs themselves tended to be short and the rhythm complex and agitated. They accompanied their song with drums, rattles, bells, horns, plucked string instruments, and xylophones.

African Music in North America

In the new environment these African songs had to serve new functions and were gradually changed to fit the new situation. Pure African songs changed their significance as blacks, no longer free, were forced to submit to the white master's authority, to accept the God of their conquerors, to put away their African instruments, especially the drums. As the white master attempted to forbid aspects of the black culture, particularly music, the blacks changed their music to a form that was more acceptable to the "massah." One song so adapted was "Swing Low, Sweet Chariot." Le-Roi Jones gives an account of the adaptation process:

> Maude Cuney-Hare, in her early book, *Negro Musicians and Their Music,* cites the experience of a Bishop Fisher of Calcutta who traveled to Central Africa . . . in Rhodesia he had heard natives sing a melody so closely resembling "Swing Low, Sweet Chariot" that he felt he had found it in its original form: moreover, the region near the great Victoria Falls have a custom from which the song arose. When one of the chiefs, in the old days, was about to die, he was placed in a great canoe together with trappings that marked his rank, and food for his journey. The canoe was set afloat in midstream headed toward the great Falls and the vast column of mist that rises from them. Meanwhile the tribe on the shore would sing its chant

of farewell. The legend is that on one occasion the king was seen to rise in his canoe at the very brink of the Falls and enter a chariot, that, descending from the mists, bore him aloft. This incident gave rise to the words "Swing Low, Sweet Chariot," and the song, brought to America by African slaves long ago, became anglicized and modified by their Christian faith.[2]

However, the details of the process by which the spirituals evolved from the slaves' work songs in America are hazy. Perhaps when blacks stopped thinking of themselves as captives and realized that they were slaves, they responded by moving away from the secular work song that satisfied needs of free people in the fields toward music of a more directly emotional and religious spirit. Jones notes that the Afro-American spirituals became much more melodic and musical than the African work songs and shouts, but that the new Afro-American spirituals could serve also as work songs.

Eventually, under the pressure of white evangelists' efforts to convert slaves to Christianity, blacks picked up key words and ideas of Christianity and incorporated them into their singing. The religion of future rewards that blacks could share with their master had powerful attraction for blacks who felt they would be slaves forever in the new world. Blacks began to adapt biblical references in songs. Fredrick Law Olmsted wrote about this adaptation of Christianity in 1856:

> A goodly proportion of them, I am told, "profess religion," and are received into the fellowship of the churches; but it is evident, of the greater part of even these, that their idea of religion, and the standard of morality which they deem consistent with a "profession" of it, is very degraded. That

they are subject to intense excitements, often really maniacal, which they consider to be religious, is true; but as these are described, I cannot see they indicate anything but a miserable system of superstition, the more painful that it employs some forms and words connected with true Christianity.[3]

Despite the changes to accommodate a new situation, blacks maintained many old African musical practices. Songs were sung by a group, as in Africa, responsorially, spontaneously, and spiritedly, usually improvised and never the same way twice. Blacks concentrated on the Christian church as a "legal" place to use up the huge emotional and spiritual reservoir dammed up by the experience of slavery. Through shouts, often the formal ring shout ceremony, blacks maintained their African heritage under the guise of a white man's religion. The ring shout was often held furtively after an official church service. Northern black teacher Charlotte Forten described one such service on the South Carolina Sea Islands in the early 1860s:

These "shouts" are very strange—in truth, almost indescribable. It is necessary to hear and see in order to have any clear idea of them. The children form a ring, and move around in a kind of shuffling dance, singing all the time. Four or five stand apart, and sing very energetically, clapping their hands, stamping their feet, and rocking their bodies to and fro. These are the musicians, to whose performance the shouters keep perfect time. The grown people did not shout, but they do on some other plantations. It is very comical to see little children not more than three or four years old, entering into performance with all their might. But the shouting of the grown people is rather solemn and impressive than otherwise. We cannot determine whether it has a religious character or not. But as the shouts of the group are always in connection with their religious meetings, it is probable that they are the barbarous expression of religion handed down to them from their African ancestors, and destined to pass away under the influence of Christian teaching.[4]

African Music in South America

The transfer of African musical materials to Latin and South American and to the Caribbean countries is a somewhat different story. Here, the details of the transfer process are more observable than in North America. Africanisms in the black religious music of Latin American countries have survived in practices which are much closer to the African originals. One reason for this difference in African survivals in North and South America is that the transfer of African musical materials to the United States occurred under circumstances that necessitated covert retention and reinterpretation. Africanisms were not allowed in American churches. In contrast, the transfer of African musical materials to Latin and South America and to the Caribbean occurred in an overt fashion. The Roman Catholic Church in these countries allowed blacks to accommodate African practices to keep them in the church.

In Brazil African culture has constantly had to seek means of expression under the cover of European traditions. This fact destroys the myth, created by apologists for the system, that racism has not existed in that country. However, the Portuguese slave system differed from that of the Spanish, English, and American in that it allowed certain African styles to live in the

New World more or less intact. Despite the inhumanities of slavery, Portuguese masters and especially the priests allowed the slaves to continue many of their traditions, including musical ones. At first the slaves lived among themselves with minimal contact with whites. African marriages were sanctioned by the church. Portuguese masters seemed to respect the African culture. Thus along with the basic conjugal family, the basic African cultural fabric remained intact.

Despite these gratuities on the part of white masters and priests, black Africans in Brazil faced a difficult struggle to maintain their African culture. That struggle often involved resourceful forms of cultural survival under the very eyes of the ethnocentric master class. Lacking either the means or consciousness to liberate themselves, the slaves resisted with the cultural weapons at hand, and scored subtle victories beyond the awareness of the masters. Often music served their purpose.

The fact that meaning in African languages varies with alterations in speaking pitch became an important cultural weapon. In the Zulu language, for example, the word *inyanga* can mean either the *moon,* or *mensuration,* or the *mouth* or a *doctor* simply by varying the tonal inflection or pitch. No change of form by prefixes or suffixes is required. Although the context of the word in the sentence may strongly suggest meaning, accent on the "wrong" syllable may result in weird ideas and hidden meanings communicated only to those who are "in the know."

These subtle melodic and speech elements are always present in Afro-Brazilian work songs such as "Pulling in the Nets" *(Puxada da Rêde).* This song is performed on the beach by fishermen who incant the gods, especially Yemanja, goddess of the sea, along with Christian saints. The song is often accompanied by a drum or two, or a rattle, and rarely a flute. The slow measured drum beats in the beginning reflect the anticipatory muscular tension as the fishermen begin the hard task of hauling in the catch. The pace mounts in volume and intensity as the nets get heavier and nearer the shore. Loud jubilant drums and voices ring out as the nets are dragged onto the sand with the fish tumbling out. Here is a typical cantico to the mother of waters *(mæ d'água):* [5]

and a cantico to Yêmanjá:

The rich rhythmic consciousness of the African brought about the transport of a large family of percussion instruments to the new world. These instruments have come to play such an integral role in Brazilian and international music and in the musical sensibilities of millions of people that we should know at least the more influential ones heard daily in Brazil. Certain African cultural material resonates through these instruments which communicate the African sense of harmony with nature. These percussion instruments are the basic tools of African religious sound.

The most important group of instruments used in religious ceremonies is the drum family. The *mangonguê* is a small cylinder drum played with the palms in liturgical street dramas as well as in popular dances. The *tarol* is a cylinder drum with a tourniquet head used in religious cycle-dramas like the nativity pastorals. The *zabumba* is a large cylinder drum played with sticks in a large number of folk dances from religious backgrounds. The *thetambu* is a large trunk drum and the *ingome* is a barrel drum, both used in the *candomblé* religious rites (religious ceremonies of communicating with the dead). The *atabaque* conical drums are also used in the *candomblé* rites. The *cuica,* a curious cylinder drum to whose membrane a chord is fixed and rubbed with wet fingers producing a frictional squeak that rises in pitch and timbre, is used in animated pieces of religious or secular music that have onomatopoetic sounds of animals. Other important instruments include the *agogo* bells, used in Afro-Brazilian magico-religious rites, especially the *candomblé;* the *marimba,* a resonant xylophone; and the various rattles that play conjurational roles in *candomblé* rites. All of these instruments play important roles in Afro-Brazilian religious cults of all kinds.

With the exception of some minor exchanges of cultural material between Bahian blacks and blacks from the Benin area in present-day Nigeria, the development of African styles in Brazil was independent of the development of African styles in Africa. Under the social circumstances of Brazil, which were radically different from those of Africa, black slaves made contacts with members of a number of different African ethnics. But, whenever possible, the Congolese slaves would regroup along the totemic clan lines of former days. In this way, various reminiscent rituals developed, such as the *congo,* which was a semi-liturgical drama that reenacted the coronation of former kings and queens of the Congo. Colonial authorities, anxious to discourage black group solidarity, attempted to exploit this provincialism among the slaves in the hopes of maintaining old African antagonisms in the compounds. However, under the pressure of slavery the blacks eventually tended to unite under their common conditions and to forget old antagonisms. Reflecting this new black solidarity, the congolese *maracatu,* a dramatic dance in the North East State of Pernambuco, evolved into a synthetic form with many totemic religious and folk motifs from the various tribes. Another interesting example of this syncretism is the *calunga,* a vestige of the Angolan and Bantu past. Calunga is either a wooden doll or a doll-like masquerade representing the goddess of the sea and fresh waters.[6]

Text: "Olele, Olele, Olele, Calunga raises her hand, to hold on Calunga, Olele, Olele."

Many African tribes were represented in Bahia, but predominant were the two Sudanese tribes who brought the *Gêge-Nago* fetish cults. In Bahia the various African fetish cults established open-air or large salon temples *(rerreiros)* for the *candomblé* ceremony.[7] The *candomblé* liturgy became syncretized to a great degree among the blacks. Its powerful music and dance became corrupted in the new environs.

The merging of the African cults with European and indigenous cultures and, in modern times, the further alterations through industrial urbanization make the tracing of the historical contours back to African origins difficult. Acculturation has necessarily meant deculturalization. While some of the cults still use the Nago and Horuban languages, for example, others use Portuguese and have been influenced by foreign elements. Such is the case with the *candomblé*.

The religious syncretization of the African cults with Catholicism in Brazil is significant. Forced by colonial persecution to find a new "respectability" for their worship, the black slaves tried to merge aspects of their religion with those of Roman Catholicism. One of the most important means of camouflaging their mythology under Christian guise was to associate their various deities with Catholic counterparts. Moreover, African and Catholic beliefs were on a common meeting ground in that the intimate personal attitudes of Catholics toward the intercession of the saints paralleled the African worship of interceding ancestors. In the mixing of African cults with Catholicism, Fango, African god of thunder and lightning, whose fetish is the meteorite, merges with the fiery archangel Michael. Yansa, African goddess of storms, merges with the protector against evil weather, St. Barbara. Oxala, godson of the high god, merges with Jesus Christ; Yêmanijá, mother over the waters, with the maternal St. Mary; Ogun, god of the hunt and metallurgy, with the militant St. George; and Exu or Leba, a demonic god, with Satan.

The Africans thus showed much resourcefulness in adapting European styles as modes of expression. The forces of syncretism not only fragmented many African styles but also concealed them among white European and American Indian elements in the developing Brazilian folk culture. For example, the Portuguese had transported to Brazil many rich pastorals (*autos*), liturgical plays that evolved from medieval miracle plays depicting the lives of the saints and biblical allegories. The Africans especially adapted the natal and paschal motifs from the Christmas and Easter cycles.

One of the most widespread and dramatic examples of this acculturated form is the "Beware of the Bull" *(bumba-meu-boi)* rite. This rite is an adaptation of a Brazilian-Portuguese rite that has historical roots in the medieval animal plays given at Christmas time. In the Afro-Brazilian version of the drama the chorus announces the arrival of a horse or man who dances comically until he is ordered to go to the bull. The bull, a full realistic body mask with fabric stretched over a wooden frame, arrives dancing the *bahian,* an Afro-Bahian dance with agitated step patterns. After the bull causes general confusion and panic, he either "dies" of exhaustion or is "stabbed" by one Mateus, who usually then hides. A doctor or healer arrives and attends the dead bull. Often, in litany form, a ceremonial butchering takes place. The various body parts, heart, liver, tripe, testicles, and hooves are mentioned and offered to people in the audience and chorus. Finally, after many magic incantations and tempting offers of money and food, the bull resurrects. The ceremony ends with the company dancing in a circle, singing good fortune to one another. The "Beware of the Bull" drama became a principal ceremonial in the cattle cycle of Brazil's northeastern folk history and is very reminiscent of the Bantu cattle culture.

African Soul-Rhythm

Africans brought to the United States and to Latin America the fundamental sounds and gestures, the essence of their African culture. This essence is soul-rhythm, the substance of music-dance. Soul-rhythm draws its strength from percussive rhythms produced by percussion instruments. These instruments create soul-sound vibrations that are much more than tympanic experiences. They are a sound event that vibrates the entire human body, abdomen, cranium, and other parts of the body and skeleton. The pacing may also resonate with human heartbeat and respiration rate. These vital vibrations are fundamental to the African sense of harmony with nature, with life, with the deities. They are genuine soul-rhythm vibrations, indeed!

The African's music begins with a metronomic motion, laying down a foundation of percussive polyrhythm, syncopating the monotony, and weaving in and out of this beating structure threads of simple, improvisational melody. It is an economic sound unit rooted in the simple dialectics of the body and the earth, life and death. No wonder it survived the cruel onslaught of feudalism, colonialism, and capitalism!

In recent years academia has seen the development of a new field known as human ecology. Founded by Robert Park and carried on by men such as McKenzie and Bews, human ecology studies the "fundamental biological triad": man, environment, and interaction. Human ecology has been most successfully applied to sociology and social stratification in particular. Kenneth Boulding has applied it to economics in his *The Organizational Revolution*. It would seem that the human ecology paradigm could profitably be applied to a study of African soul-rhythm and the influences of man, environment, and interaction. The results of such a study could aid our endeavors to fight racism and to come to new inter- and intra-cultural understandings.

4

"Soul" Music
of the Black Community

The 1960s witnessed the declaration of black identity in America, the association of black Americans with black Africa, and the recognition by blacks of their African musical heritage and of the transfer of these African sounds and beats to the Americas. These new perspectives provide insights into the capacity of American black music to evoke in listeners and participants a fervent response that may sometimes approach ecstasy—a kind of musical religious "trip." By religious music I do not refer only to the traditional terms of sacred music, but also to unorthodox types of religious music, in fact all music, *musica humana,* that may arouse spiritual fervor and heighten religious experience. All music may serve as a channel through which truth can be imparted and through which believers may devote themselves to greater service to God and humanity. All music may deepen a religious experience, may help to brighten every aspect, every sentiment of human life. Black culture in America expresses this capacity of *musica humana* to arouse and to inspire as *soul*.

What is soul music? What is soul?

Black Soul

Black soul as it is understood in black and white America stands for active blackness. Jones has written, "The step to soul is a form of social aggression. . . . It is an attempt to reverse the social roles within the society by redefining the canons of value."[1] Jones' poem "Black Dada Nihilism" dramatizes the growth of militant black power, that is of soul, in the United States by alternating scenes of black life with the chorus-like chant: "black, black dada nihilism." This chant refrain mocks everything and anything that blacks may hold sacred. "Black is not beautiful; black is nothing," he chants mockingly. He directs the poem at a white audience. Thus he calls attention to America's long history of mocking blackness. He is really saying, "Black is nothing—*now*. What are you going to do about it?"

Through soul, blacks, especially the ghetto dwellers, have begun to transvalue black identity from "black as nothing" to "black as beautiful." Still the question remains: what specifically does "soul" mean? The term "soul" has perhaps its greatest utility and its tenderest vulnerability in that it has, in fact, no single meaning. Charles Keil in his *Urban Blues* wrote that "to milk this word for all its meaning . . . we must construct a catalogue of Negro culture."[2] Even if soul suffers, as Jones believes it does, from the absence of any universal denotative function, still, so long as soul refers to some essentially undefinable identity in which all blacks share, it functions as an inclusive rather than an exclusive identity. Every black has soul; no black need fear exclusion. If, however, the term were defined in terms of specific criteria, its capacity as an inclusive all-embracing symbol for the essence of blackness would be severely threatened. The choice of the very term *soul* suggests both universality and indefinability by its association with the term defined in the religious sense as a spiritual part of man. Black soul seems to have overtones of meaning borrowed from the religious concept by the same name. Just as every individual has a soul in the religious sense, every black person has black soul. Soul in both the black and religious senses refers to a spiritual part of man which is distinct from his physical being and immune to physical attack.

Gradually, the social aggression (to use Jones' term) associated with soul has taken a more direct approach exemplified by the rhetoric of "black is beautiful." It is only, however, within the last decade that the concept of soul has broadened to encompass "the entire catalogue of Negro culture." Initially, soul was associated only with black music and musicians. This close tie between black soul and black music reflects not only the importance of music in black society in America but also black awareness of the potential of soul as music for providing a sense of black identity and even for breaking social barriers and eroding racist attitudes.

Of all the aspects of black culture, only its music has consistently found eager acceptance outside of the black community. In fact, it seems sometimes that this music has found acceptance despite its blackness. For example, black musical styles such as the blues, jazz, and today's soul music have attracted large and enthusiastic white audiences. Moreover, most white enthusiasts for this music are at least vaguely aware of the creation of this popular music by black musicians, or at least of the deep involvement of black musicians in its performances. The black faces of such great black musicians as Louis Armstrong, Ella Fitzgerald, Ray Charles, and Aretha Franklin occupy a prominent spot in the picture of American popular culture.

By comparison, the important role that black musicians have played in American church music is a comparatively unknown story. So is the fact that the creative process for much American hymnody included popular music. Many white church leaders who cling proudly and tenaciously to "their" gospel hymnody are apparently unaware of the black and popular origins of their favorite gospel songs. They may resist the introduction of jazz and rock music into their churches while supporting special choirs devoted only to the performance of gospel hymnody. This situation constitutes one of the great ironies of our story.

Yet, even while black music poured into the mainstream of American white society through radio, television, and the recording industry, and while white musicians unconsciously adopted the black style of church music for their own, most blacks have continued to occupy the lowest strata of American society. Not only did most of them never see the inside of a middle-class home or church; many of them never saw beyond the walls of the urban ghettos in which they were born, lived, and died. Music was the only vital link between those within and without the walls. Thus soul's initial association with black music was a force to chip away at the walls of the urban ghetto, and ultimately to help change white society's perception of the value of blacks.

The promulgation of soul in white society, an image for a distinct black lifestyle and culture, has helped many white Americans change their negative stereotypes of blacks. For example, whites can readily identify with aspects of soul that parallel aspects of their own ethnic identity. The development of soul language and food parallels areas of white ethnic pride and identification. Black soul language, while clearly not the language of an "old country," has its own vocabulary and inflection. In "soul" English words may take on new meanings as they are spoken among soul brothers and sisters. For whites, hearing soul language on the bus is in some ways like hearing any foreign language. The strange sounds of the other language bring about a certain sense of isolation; in this sense, blacks have turned the table—white listeners are the outsiders, the excluded. Clothing styles have a similar effect. Afro-hairdos and shirts and dresses made of bright colored African prints are signs of pride in blackness. Some whites try self-consciously to break the barrier to soul by adopting an Afro-hairstyle or Afro-clothing.

Through the image of soul, many blacks identify themselves as a group with the same terms used to identify and describe ethnic groups. While the analogy between soul and ethnicity has its limits, it has been useful in helping blacks to find a place within the mainstream of American society. Yet soul has its own strong characteristics. It is not historically but socially motivated. It begins with the ecstatic and aggressive music of American blacks, subproletarian and superexploited in white America. In a sense, soul music expresses the blacks' consciousness of non-Americanness while living and working in America, at the same time that it enables blacks to begin living on the same terms as other Americans. Through soul, blacks express that they have been unlike other Americans, and at the same time that they are like them for this reason. Blacks have lived and worked in America and have been freed to live separately. Ironically, consciousness of African roots seems to enable blacks to be like other

51

Americans. In these ways, soul sets the black society in America apart to gather strength for social aggression.

Even if black social aggression is a painstakingly slow process, soul serves in the meantime to provide a positive self-image for the large majority of black persons who find themselves still tightly locked behind the walls of the urban ghetto. Soul helps to free the black urban ghetto dweller from guilt about his apparent failure to find escape from economic and social oppression. He finds ideals in the vague concept of soul, which has its own values apart from those of the mainstream of American society. Through soul, the black urban ghetto dweller has dignified every aspect of his life. He possesses his own soul culture—language, food, art, and lifestyle. Through soul he has begun to dispel what W. E. B. DuBois once called "A peculiar sensation . . . this sense of always looking at one's self through the eyes of others, of measuring one's soul by the tape of a world that looks on in amused contempt and pity." [3] Being a soul brother or sister is *not* belonging to a group that does not measure up by the Anglo-American tape. Being a soul brother or sister is belonging to a group that measures with its own tape!

The association of soul with black identity is not a new idea. What is new is the blossoming of soul into a widely shared sense of black identity. As early as 1903, W. E. B. DuBois published a series of essays titled *The Souls of Black Folk* in which he tried to explore "the strange meaning of being black . . . to sketch, in vague, uncertain outline, the spiritual world in which ten thousand Americans live and strive." [4] These essays were reprinted in 1961, the twenty-sixth edition, not counting the many European editions. In the introduction for the 1961 edition, Saunders Redding described the reactions to the work of DuBois from black readers who felt that DuBois gave them "words with which to voice . . . Negro-ness." [5]

In this work DuBois underlined the capacity of the black soul to speak through music by introducing each of the essays with a bit of text and music from one of the black spirituals. In the final essay, "Of the Sorrow Songs," he discussed the spirituals and also explained his reason for using musical captions throughout the book:

> They that walked in darkness sang songs in the olden days—Sorrow Songs—for they were weary at heart. And so before each thought that I have written in this book I have set a phrase, a haunting echo of these weird old songs in which the soul of the black slave spoke to men. [6]

Although what we know today as "soul" music has developed a new musical vocabulary quite different from that of the slave spirituals, today's blacks continue to live in a society in which they feel dispossessed. DuBois spoke of the veil that separated blacks from America. Since the beginning of their American experience, blacks have cried out their sense of desperation and alienation in music—spiritual, gospel song, blues, jazz, and now soul. The message seems to be always the same.

Today's term *soul music* stands for self-identification of the black singer as is illustrated in the performance of Aretha Franklin, Lady Soul. Through her gospel songs she gives powerful expression to her own feelings; her self-expression brings fulfillment to the blacks' need to be heard. DuBois expressed this need in the language of prayer and pleading in his "After Thought" to *The Souls of Black Folk*.

> Hear my cry, O God the reader; vouchsafe that this my book fall not stillborn into the world

wilderness. Let there spring, Gentle One, from out its leaves vigor of thought and thoughtful deed to reap the harvest wonderful. Let the ears of a guilty people tingle with truth, and seventy millions sigh for the righteousness which exalteth nations, in this drear day when human brotherhood is mockery and a snare. Thus in Thy good time may infinite reason turn the tangle straight, and these crooked marks on a fragile leaf be not indeed.[7]

The blacks have been heard through their great singers. Still today blacks speak through their songs. Black singers do not stay in a mold assigned by white society. They refuse to please when they do not want to entertain or to be helped. Black singers express the desperation of the black community. In her performance of "Don't Let Me Lose This Dream," Aretha Franklin pleads with her listeners:

> If I lose this dream I don't know what I'm gonna do,
> If it goes away, I might as well hang it up.
> I only know that if I lose, it's goodbye love and happiness.

Through their black singers blacks have also felt the respect and recognition they crave and deserve. Writing in 1963 LeRoi Jones in his *Blues People* stated his belief that the black blues are the only significant American contribution to western culture.

The Black Spiritual

Soul is as old as the plight of the blacks in foreign America. The spirituals, or *sorrow songs* as DuBois called them, show the basic ingredients of today's soul culture. Like soul the spiritual can be understood within the concept of *musica humana*. Like soul the spiritual has many meanings. First, the spiritual is a song of soul-nostalgia sung by persons forced to live in a foreign land. The feeling of being still in an alien world has parallels in the feelings of the black slave for the Christian religion forced on him. He heard preachings of a Christian faith that related the rightness of his low estate to the placidness of saintliness and the necessity of an obedient life. Through his spirituals he showed, however, that he did not accept the message of obedience but rather heard the story of the children of Israel who were enslaved in a foreign land, and who, one day, had been delivered from bondage. He sang of Moses, a man who fought the slave system and won.

When Israel was in Egypt's land,
    Let my people go.
Oppressed so hard they could not stand,
    Let my people go.
Go down, Moses, way down to Egypt's land,
Tell old Pharaoh, let my people go.

Reminiscences of former slaves and the accretion of legend and hearsay have pinpointed Harriet Tubman, the Negro antislavery worker and unofficial "conductor" of the Underground Railroad, as the living "Moses" of this song.

The spiritual is also a song of soul freedom. It revealed the black's religious belief in freedom, which provided a sense of internal freedom through religious expression, a belief that the spiritual part of man will survive the physical one, a true soul concept. His belief also provided a sense of freedom from physical bonds. Ultimately his belief replaced the passivity preached by the white Christian preachers with activism. Finally there was freedom in the one event which makes all men equal—death itself.

The black man's religion was not organized. He usually attended a Baptist or a Methodist church with his master on the plantation or in separated quarters in the town church. But this formal church experience had little to do with his religion. His true religion belonged to his precious time alone, the brief hours when he was not working. It was then that he could talk, pray, and sing as he wished. He met with other slaves in secret to express his real belief, and as the Civil War drew to a close, to hear reports of impending freedom. The freedom he felt within himself during these few brief moments gave birth within him, in his soul, to the idea, the belief, that he was fitted for a better life, a life which would come sooner than the white master ever dreamed. He sang:

> I'm a sometimes up and sometimes down;
>   Oh yes, Lawd!
> But still my soul feel heaven bound,
>   Oh yes, Lawd!

The spiritual is also a soul- work-song of men living under forced labor conditions. They are not only work songs in a literal sense, but they came from the soul, the center of being. The blues mood of "Take Dis Hammer" does not disguise the pick, shovel, grubbing hoe, sledge or pick hammer rhythm and movement of the song. Nor does the spiritual addressed to the deity of "Swing Low, Sweet Chariot" mask the movement of the cotton-picker's lunge against the shoulder strap of his ten-foot cotton sack, nor does it mask the song's adaptability to the rhythm of chopping cotton, cutting cane, or matching a mule's steps in pulling a double shove. "Sink 'em low," "Michael row de boat ashore," "Mammy rockin' Li'l Martha," and "Black sheep" are all examples of work songs full of soul, full of spirituality embodying the soul and the spirit of the black man in slavery.

Finally, the spiritual is also a soul-protest song. In the spiritual lullaby "Black Sheep," the black sheep has left her lamb in the pasture, that is, the field, where "the buzzards and flies are peckin' out his eyes, and de po' li'l lamb say Mammy!" "Dere's a man goin' round takin' names" may be a song about the Lamb's Book of Life, a fact important to the destiny of the black; but the man is also like a master picking out a few slaves to be sold, or perhaps to be whipped because they have fallen below the master's standards in their forced labor, something much more important to the black's immediate situation. In "Oh, Mary don' yer weep," the singer says, "Don't know what my mother stays here fer; dis worl' ain't very good to her." "Nobody knows de trouble I see" is quite a familiar protest spiritual. "Take dis hammer, O Lord, and carry it to de captain" is an expression in blues of what Jesus felt when he said, "Lord, if it is thy will, let this cup pass from me."

The Blues

The blues is also a song of *musica humana,* of soul-protest and of soul-freedom. Its message is more directly spoken than that of the spirituals. After the Civil War, when blacks were "free" and were thrust into urban situations or on small farms, the group expression of common spirit necessarily declined because the large plantation was declining. Slowly, blues replaced the spiritual as the dominant musical expression. Whereas the spiritual is tied to a land-based agrarian society, the blues came with the mobile ur-

57

ban society. Li'l Son Jackson spoke of the distinction between the spiritual and the blues: "You see, it's two things. If a man feel hurt within side and he sing a church song, then he's askin' God for help. It's a horse of a different color, but I think if a man sing the blues, it's more or less out of himself. . . . He's not askin' no one for help." [8] The soul quality in the blues is in the strength, power, and beauty of the musical expression found by the individual black as he addresses himself as an individual to the group.

Gospel Songs

The same depth of expression of the individual to the group wandered from the blues to the Afro-American gospel songs, the black *musica humana* of our time. The gospel singer's feeling of rage at the adversities and frustration of poverty and racial prejudice give the gospel song its characteristic future. The great gospel singers began life poor and black in white America and remember years of bitter struggle. At age twelve Julius Cheeks picked cotton in South Carolina. Mahalia Jackson worked as a nursemaid for white families in New Orleans. Marion Williams scrubbed floors in Florida. Dorothy Love washed dishes in Alabama. Gospel provided the one way out of the poverty and violence that marked their lives, a way of warding off despair and hopelessness and gaining the courage to carry on. Gospel music was one of the few ways of "making it," of acquiring money and recognition.

But the gospel highway is one of the toughest and most dangerous routes in show business. Violence and tragedy pervade many lives. Robbers have murdered "Chip" Harris, lead singer of the old Norfolk Jubilee Quartet. Sam Cooke was slain in a back room brawl. Myrtle Jackson was shot by a sniper as she came out of church. One of Bessie Griffin's pianists was found dead in the oven of a deserted tenement.[9] Gospel singers are frequently asked to sing at funerals of old, close friends who have been killed tragically. In the span of a few months Marion Williams sang at the funerals of an old fan stabbed to death, a former coworker's brother killed in a gang fight, and a good friend's nephew who had died of an overdose of heroin.[10]

As a result gospel songs are filled with images of paranoia and of the ugliness of ghetto life. They are testimonies of everyday life experiences, trials, tribulations, troubles. Their greatest soul quality is that they are filled with black anger, black pride, and black power. Reverend Brewster exhibited black pride back in the 1930s when he named Q. C. Anderson after Queen Candace of Ethiopia.[11] In the 1940s quartets sang "No Separation in Heaven." Dorothy Love and Julius Cheeks have been speaking out for civil rights and against the lynchings, bombings, and segregated facilities since the early 1950s.[12] But most important of all the gospel traditions is its human quality to sustain and nourish millions of black people. In their own church and through their own music, soul-qualities of the spiritual, of nostalgia, and of freedom have become a part of their gospel sound. Black men and women have been able to speak with dignity and authority, establish a sense of personal worth, and regain hope that they will surely overcome some day.[13]

The Black Worship Service

Soul is very much in evidence in the worship services of black congregations in the communal dialog (not necessarily call-response) of the liturgy and its music.

The musical role of the black preacher is often

fraternal, involving an equalitarian sharing with members of his congregation. Often the sermon delivery will have characteristics of the performance of certain blues: the pastor will intone and recite part or all of his sermon, with the congregation interjecting shouts, moans, and various comments. In fact, some blues singers, on conversion, give up blues and become preachers, though retaining some of the aspects of blues performance practice. For many members of the congregation the blues may be the Saturday night prelude to the Sunday morning service. The musical vocabulary of the blues deeply permeates every aspect of musical experience for the black community. Moreover, popularization of the blues in the white community by such figures as Ray Charles has resulted in the promulgation of this music by the media.

Thus for the black person, the sense of fragmentation between daily music and Sunday music may be minimal. The texts of the black liturgies often refer directly to the relevant social, political, and racial issues of the day. A violent race riot motivated W. E. B. DuBois to prepare his "Litany of Atlanta (In the Day of Death)" in 1906.

READER: To whom do we pray? Is not the God of our creation dead? Have not seers seen in Heaven's Halls Thy lifeless form stark amidst the black and rolling smoke of sin, where all along bow bitter forms of endless death?

RESPONSE: Where are you God that sleepest?

READER: Thou are not dead, but flown afar, up hills of endless light, through blazing corridors of suns, where worlds do swing with good and gentle men, with women strong

and free—far from deceit, hypocrisy and
chaste prostitution of this shameful speck
of dust?

RESPONSE: Turn again toward us, oh Lord. Leave us
not to perish in our sin.

While a communal-dialog liturgy is typical for black
churches, the specific liturgical plan may vary greatly
from one black church to the next. LeRoi Jones emphasized that black society is stratified, and the music
reflects this stratification. Vattel Daniel in his study of
"Ritual and Stratification in Chicago Negro Churches"
pointed out that the various strata of black society
are served by different types of church in which particular liturgies are used, liturgies which not only engage the participants in the community of Christianity,
but also serve distinct social needs. For example, the
liturgies of the black middle-class church may approach the restrained and self-conscious atmosphere
of white middle-class churches, and worshippers who
interrupt the service with singing and shouting may
even be removed from the service.

The communal participation common in most black
liturgies counteracts the sense of alienation and lack
of identity which many blacks experience in the larger
white society. Participation in the communal liturgy
may afford the black churchgoer a precious sense of
a clearly defined role. In liturgical participation, the
alienated black of the disadvantaged stratum temporarily steps out of the insecure isolation of his daily
existence. Vattel Daniel correlates the ecstatic behavior
prevalent in certain black sects with extreme social
isolation.

The ecstatic drive of soul music is present in some
of the liturgies of the black church. They are often
characterized by emotional appeal, informality, and

61

community emphasis on individual faith and experience, equalitarian ideals, and a lay clergy. A marvelous example of soul ecstasy through total participation of leader and congregation, shouting, feet stomping, and hand clapping was recorded at the State Prison Farm at Jennings, Louisiana in 1934.[14]

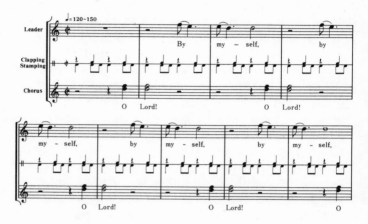

5

"Soul" Music Qualities
in European-American Culture

The question, "What is music?" has elicited at least
as many answers as there are musical styles. In the
first century the Roman Quintilianus thought music
was the science of melody. St. Augustine in the fifth
century believed that music was the science of changing sounds in a beautiful way—*bene modulandi*. The
sixth century theorist Cassiodorus believed that music
was a discipline involving numerical relationships. The
men of the Renaissance and Reformation era saw music
in the light of musical performance practice; music
was the art of *how to perform* correctly, rightly, beau-
tifully. Rationalistic and enlightened 18th century men
usually saw music as both a science and an art. Charles
Burney, the historical music annotator of this period,
described music as "an innocent luxury, unnecessary
indeed, to our existence, but a great improvement and
gratification to our sense of hearing." In the 19th century Romantic music was viewed as a natural force
to help people express sentiments through sound and
even as a means to moral improvement.

The Mutability of Church Music

This brief and necessarily incomplete survey of the changing meanings of music should shatter any illusions we might have about the immutability of music, even church music. Music has not always been as it is, nor has it always meant what it means today. Similarly, church music has not always been as it is, nor has it always been seen as something mysteriously inspired by "Divine Ventriloquism." [1] That church music and what it means has changed and is changing is a fact; that it will change is inevitable.

The church, however, has not been without influence or passive in the development of music. Throughout the centuries, the church has exerted a powerful influence on the course of the history of western music. Western music has its very roots in the music of the Hebraic religion. The Roman and Greek Catholic Churches assimilated and adapted many of the Hebraic musical practices to create the corpus of chant in the early Christian church. The early church further contributed enormously to the history of western classical music in its gift of the immensely complex and sophisticated Gregorian chant. The chant then generated the birth of polyphonic art music that developed during the Gothic and Renaissance eras into a unique musical manifestation of man's ability to express his faith through highly diversified organizations and structures of sound.

Music and Transcendence

The church has never lost its interest in music. Over the centuries music has served as a rich ornament of the church. The church, however, has not only been interested in the ornamental aspects of music. More important for the church's purposes has been the capacity of music to transport man beyond his physical self and surroundings into the realm of the spiritual.

The idea of music as a means to spiritual transcendence is probably as old as music itself. Writing in the fourth century B.C., Aristotle made a distinction in his *Politics* between "enthusiastic" and "ethical" and "practical" music. Aristotle's "enthusiastic" music served as a catharsis because it allowed man to plunge into an emotional and soulful outburst of feelings. Writing seven centuries later, St. Augustine also described a kind of musical catharsis when he wrote:

> How did I cry about the hymns and [spiritual] songs [dedicated] to you, moved powerfully by the harmony of these songs of your church! The tunes penetrated into my ear and truth floated into my heart, a feeling of piety and intimacy gushed over me: tears were streaming, and I felt at ease.[2]

In more recent history, Dietrich Bonhoeffer described a soulful effect of music in his *Letters and Papers from Prison*. He felt, for example, that concentrated listening to Beethoven's piano sonata, Opus 111, yielded a musical purity previously unimagined. The effect on the soul of the person who apprehends and incorporates this "new body" of the music could be nothing less than salutary, almost unquestionably ennobling.[3]

As we have seen in the previous chapter, black soul music seems to involve a state of soulful ecstasy similar to that described at various times throughout the history of man. In the black experience of soul music, however, there is the additional experience of spiritual identity, of belonging, of security apart from a hostile world. The specific combination of soulful ecstasy and identity through music has also served the purpose of white people. This effect of music occurred in European musical culture and especially in Euro-American musical culture among groups of persons who found themselves alienated from the mainstream of society and especially from the established church.

White Soul Music

An early instance of white soul occurred in the development of pietistic Lutheranism in 17th century Germany. The theologians of this movement, Conrad Dannhauer (1603-1666), Hector Mithobius (1631-?), Theophil Grossgebauer (1627-1661), and especially Heinrich Müller (1631-1675) even anticipated current black usage of the term soul in their discussions of the phenomenon of *Seelenmusik*—soul music. Müller identified the Holy Spirit as the singing master, the one who brings about the spiritually drunken state of ecstasy. Müller wrote:

> Ein Trunckener frolocket und jauchzet/singet und springet/für Freuden; also offenbahrt sich die Freud des Geists durch. Psalmen/Lobgesange/und geistliche Lieder: eine Geist-trunckene Seele verschleust sich offt in ihrem Kammerlein/ . . . redet als ihr wol zu muth ist. Ein Trunckener hat Lust zur Musik.[4]
>
> (An ecstatic is exalted and shouts/ sings and jumps/ with rejoicing; thus the rejoicing of the spirit is revealed. Psalms/ tunes of praise/ and spiritual songs: a soul elated with the spirit often locks itself up in its chamber/ . . . where it talks as it pleases. An ecstatic delights in music.)

The person who experiences this spirit-filled state abandons his sense of individuality and even his sense of communality and fellowship with others. Motivated

66

by great enthusiasm and powerful emotions, his song is a compulsive utterance. Although the singing is most important to this spiritually drunken state of ecstasy, this soul experience may also involve physical movements such as hand clapping and dancing.

Seelenmusik's most outstanding protagonist, Heinrich Müller, stressed the importance of singing as a preparation for involvement in the liturgy. This service of preparation, in some ways similar to that of the Eastern Orthodox rite, and preceded by a period of confession, serves to draw the heart away from the world of sin, and to bring about a complete denial of the self, to erase all awareness of the troubles of life, to bring about a sense of ecstatic tranquility in the presence of God, and acknowledgement of God's goodness, love, and justice. Müller believed that church music, in the limited sense of music for strictly liturgical times of prayer and praise, did not tend to bring about this sense of ecstatic tranquility. Neither did he believe that *Seelenmusik* had to be sung at church. "The place does not sanctify the works, but the works sanctify the place." [5] Soul singing need not be restricted to the liturgical location of the church, nor to the chamber music of the home. It is first and foremost to be found in the chamber of the heart. Thus it is truly soul music.

The 17th and 18th centuries saw the rise of several other movements similar to that of Lutheran pietism. Even as early as the 16th century the Polish Socinians emerged in opposition to both Lutheranism and Roman Catholicism in a fight for the simplification of dogma and for social justice. In the 17th and 18th centuries the Quakers in England and the Moravians in Central Europe grew out of a stress on inwardness as the key to faith.

The Jews of this period, surrounded by an ocean of

hatred, superstition, and persecution, gave birth to the great revivalist movement in Jewish history known as Hasidism. The hasidic lifestyle brought on an other-worldly ecstasy that made it possible for the Hasids in Poland and Russia to overcome unbearably anarchic social and economic conditions. For the Hasids, worshiping with spontaneity, enthusiasm *(hitlahavut)* and ecstasy became more important than the established services of the synagogue. Through prayer, song, and dance, the Hasid liberated himself in worship and drew himself toward God. The dance, above all, became a form of self-expression and a sacred service. Through their dance the Hasids approached a kind of religious ecstasy that carried them beyond their suffering physical selves and their surroundings to the highest heavens. Their dances included the Mitzvah dance and the handkerchief dance performed at weddings, as well as other dances performed on religious festivals, on the Sabbath, and on the anniversary of a *tzadik's* death. In the hasidic perspective each person through his very humanity had the means to draw himself close to God. The man in the marketplace could draw himself close to God. The man in the marketplace could draw as near to his Father in heaven as could the rabbi in his study.

The Pennsylvania Pietists

In the early years of settlement in America, groups that fled religious persecution in Europe provide striking examples of religious practices that utilized music's capacity to bring about a state of soulful ecstasy. William Penn's colony, known for its religious toleration, provided a safe haven for many such dissenting and persecuted groups that emigrated from central Europe. Among these are the Mennonites, followers of Menno Simons, who sought refuge in Pennsylvania between 1683 and 1784 in a series of migrations.

More interesting from our point of view are the Amish, a splinter-group of the Mennonites that settled in Pennsylvania under the leadership of Jacob Ammen in 1725. Although the Mennonite hymnbook in use today is not much different from any Protestant hymnbook, the Amish hymnal has retained an old and distinctive style of hymnody. They have "passed it [hymnody] on from ear to ear for more than two hundred and fifty years." [6] The Amish have traditionally clung to their customs and language. Even today the Amish in their various settlements speak a German dialect. Representative of their deep ties to the past and resistance to the changing world outside of their settlements are their recent battles over the issue of the education of their children and what they see as threats to their lifestyle from state laws regarding child education. In the foreword to the first Amish hymnal *Amische Lieder,* published in 1942 at Huntington, Pennsylvania, editor Joseph W. Yoder clearly stated the Amish "principle that 'change' is not desirable" and that through the hymnal publication he hoped "to preserve their music." [7]

The Amish hymns are of two types, slow hymns *(langsame Weise)* and strong hymns *(stärke Weise).* The slow hymns are often highly embellished versions of well-known melodies including many Lutheran chorales. Such an embellished style of singing thrived naturally in the Amish communities that kept their hymnody alive through oral tradition and made no efforts toward musical literacy. Despite the Amish opposition to change, Yoder admitted in 1942, "Some leaders who have traveled about find that there is considerable difference in different communities in the singing of these hymns." [8]

The Amish version of the favorite chorale, "Wachet auf," (Sleepers, Awake) illustrates this embellishment:[9]

Wachet auf.

(Erst Lied am Tisch.)

K'funge bei dem
Christian S. Yoder
und gebilligt bei dem
Reuben Kauffman, 1910.

D. B. 238

1. Wa — chet auf ruft uns die Stim — me
2. Zi — on hört die Wäch — ter fin — gen,
3. Glo — ri — a fei dir ge — fun — gen,

Der Wäch — ter fehr hoch auf der Zin — ne,
Das Herz thut ihr für Freu — den fprin — gen,
Mit Men — fchen= und mit En — gel= Zun — gen,

The initial tendency to alter the old Lutheran hymns may have arisen from a rebellion against the Lutheran standard. The dissenting Amish embroidered the old tunes into a new, elaborate, and individual musical fabric. They retained the old Lutheran melodies but in an unrecognizable form. The rational and simple Lutheran melodies lost their old identity in the complex and turgid Amish elaborations. The Amish versions of the tunes tend to twist and turn incessantly within a limited range. Their version of the first phrase of "Wachet Auf" falls entirely within a range of a fifth but involves 23 melodic movements with no melodic skips larger than a major third. Most of the melody is made up of stepwise wanderings within the short compass of the melody. This constantly meandering melodic style effectively obscures the clear tonal outline of the original melody. The simple melody as it appears in the Lutheran *Service Book and Hymnal* provides a striking contrast to the Amish version.[10]

Wake, a - wake, for night is fly - ing the
Mid - night hears the wel - come voic - es and

watch-men on the heights are cry - ing, a - wake Je - ru -
at the thrill - ing cry re - joic - es: Come forth, ye vir -

sa - lem at last! The bride - groom comes, a - wake, your
gins, night is past!

lamps with glad - ness take; Al - le - lu - ia! And for his

mar - riage feast pre - pare, for ye must go to meet him there.

Only eleven years after the first Mennonite migration to Pennsylvania, Johannes Kelpius led a group of solitaries to settle on the banks of the Wissahickon River in 1694. For Johannes Kelpius' "Contented of the God-Loving Soul," or as their Pennsylvania neighbors called them, the "Wissahickon Hermits" or "The Society of the Woman in the Wilderness" (referring to the Woman of the Revelation who prefigured deliverance in the Millenium), prayers were the only means to self-purification. Kelpius believed that the Father wished his children to be free from every fault, that Christ desired those of whom he became the victim to be purified from sin, and a virgin to be delivered to him. Kelpius wrote, "The Holy Spirit effecteth that this will of the Father and of the Son be accomplished in us as yet in this life." [11] In contrast to groups that denied the propriety of using instruments or accompanied singing in church, Kelpius utilized all instruments available, from the organ to the kettle drum. To Kelpius, music and its use was sacred because all of life is sacred, a minute-by-minute journey of purification toward ultimate self-denial and perfection. He believed music to be an integral part of life, a means to express feelings toward the Lord and to draw man to man, and man to God.

A follower of his, Justus Falckner, went still farther in the use of the organ as a means of creating feelings of brotherhood between man and feelings of proximity to God. In a report written in Germantown in 1701 to Dr. Heinrich Mühlen in Germany, Falckner pleaded for an organ, saying that the organ would attract the Indians who greatly loved music. Once they began coming to hear the music, the Indians could be taught the message of the gospel. The organ music would also attract members of other sects. He also hoped to reach the unchurched rural people who preferred to rest on Sunday rather than to make the long ride to church. Falckner believed the addition of organ music to the service would make church-going a recreation for these people and would prompt them to come.[12]

Perhaps most interesting among the Pennsylvania pietists is the settlement led by John Conrad Beissel at Ephrata. In this pietistic community known as the Ephrata Community, the purpose of their solitary orders was to elevate the soul and to glorify God. Each member of the community worked toward personal union of his soul with God. To this purpose celibacy was suggested, and a high degree of communal ownership was instituted. He who freed himself from the flesh attained the mystical union with God. Thus their colorful and famous singing master Conrad Beissel suggested strange dietary rules. He was especially interested in the spiritual virginity of his choirs and the effect of such things on the vocal chords of the solitary.

> Care must be taken of the body, and its requirements reduced to a minimum, so that the voice may become angelic, heavenly, pure and clear, and not rough and harsh through the use of coarse

food, and therefore unfit to produce the proper quality of tone. . . .

At the same time, it is especially necessary to know what kinds of food will make the spirit teachable, and the voice flexible and clear. For it is certain that all meat dishes, by whatever name known quite discommode us, and bring no small injury to the pilgrim on his way to the silent beyond. Then there are those other articles of food which we improperly derive from animals: e.g. *milk,* which causes heaviness and uneasiness; *cheese,* which produces heat and begets desire for other and forbidden things; *butter,* which makes indolent and dull and satiates to such an extent that one no longer feels the need of singing or praying; *eggs,* which arouse numerous capricious cravings; *honey,* which brings bright eyes and a cheerful spirit, but not a clear voice.

As regards the other common vegetables, none are more useful than the ordinary potato, the beet, and other tubers. Beans are too heavy, satiate too much, and are liable to arouse impure desires. Above all must it be remembered that the spirit of this exalted art, because it is a pure, chaste and virtuous spirit, suffers no unclean, polluted and sinful love for woman, which so inflames and agitates the blood of the young as completely to undo them in mind, heart, voice, and soul.[13]

The music used was of Beissel's own composition, and this was copied by the sisters. More than four hundred of Beissel's hymns were copied in the hymnbook, *Zionistischer Weyrauth's-Hügel.* Most of his music was based on the tones of the Aeolian harp. The choral singing was an imitation of Aeolian harp harmony. In 1835 William Fahnestock wrote an account of the singing, and it appears that he actually had the opportunity to hear the chorus singing:

> It is very peculiar in its style and contents, and in its execution. The tones issuing from the choir imitate very soft instrumental music, conveying a softness and devotion almost superhuman to the auditor. Their music is set in four, six, and eight parts. All the parts save the bass are lead and sung exclusively by females, the men being confined to the bass, which is set in two parts, the high and low bass—the latter resembling the deep tones of the organ, and the first, in combination with one of the female parts, is an excellent imitation of the concert horn.
>
> The whole is sung in the falsetto voice, the singers scarcely opening their mouths, or moving their lips, which throws the voice up to the ceiling, which is not high, and the tones, which seem to be more than human, at least so far from common church singing appear to be entering above, and hovering above the heads of the assembly. . . . They have nearly a thousand pieces of music, a piece being composed for every hymn. This music is lost entirely, now, at Ephrata—not the music books, but the style of singing: they never attempt it any more.[14]

The Shakers

The Shakers, a small English-American sect that emerged at the end of the 18th century, engaged themselves in religious ecstatic experiences somewhat similar to those of the Hasids. Even more than for the Jewish Hasids, the dance for the Christian Shakers was a key activity in their search for self and group identification. Through their dances, songs, hymns, psalms, and theology they rebelled against male dominion and supremacy in human and religious societies. Thus, they actually became the first modern women's liberation movement that was effectively executed as a religious and social way of life. Their theology was based on the thought of Mother Anne, their founder, who they believed embodied the Second Coming of Christ. Mother Anne was not only seen as the Bride of Jesus, but also as the one who gave love to her followers. She was thus the active incorporation of the female into a place of honor and equality. The first stanza of one of the Shaker hymns reveals the affinity between Shaker beliefs and today's women's liberation movement.

All till the women got free
Groaning was the common sound.

The second stanza of this same hymn provides justification for a female rather than male personage in the Second Coming.

Sure it could not be a man
None with Jesus could compare.

And the cry of liberation is heard in stanzas six and seven.

On the level we now stand
And are just free as you
For it is the women's day.

The "women's day" is truly exemplified in the concluding stanza in which the women unite with the men in shouts of heavenly joy.[15]

Puritan Psalm-Singing

The 17th century American Puritans left European persecution behind to found a new city on a hill. America was for the Puritans a sacred and harmonious God-given space. It had the beauty of divine love and represented order, absolute good, harmony, perfection, and unity—all the qualities toward which a Puritan strove to become an instrument of God's will and to do God's work in this sacred land. They sang the psalms as an important part of this divine work assignment. After the passing of the first generation, most of the Puritans were not able to read music because the new environment had not been conducive to musical studies.

Unable to read music, the Puritans resorted to singing their psalms by following a song leader, line by line. The leader functioned as a kind of religious specialist, as one who, being filled with the voice of God, served as an instrument through whom God called his people. The leader's state of soulfulness radiated to the assembly, which repeated the lines, often changing and embellishing the original tunes according to each individual's soulful feeling. The singing of the psalms in this fashion became an exuberant, communal, and emotional religious experience carried on in open rebellion against the orthodox liturgies of the Anglican and Roman churches. The Puritan authorities eventually came to oppose this increasingly soulful manner of psalm singing and encouraged a rational "regular" style of singing by rules.

The Revival Movement

Later in American history the revival and social reform movements in 19th century America were accompanied by a kind of soulful song. These later movements emphasized a highly personal awareness of God. According to Charles Grandison Finney (1792-1875), one of the greatest organizers of religious revivals, a pious young man "filled with the Spirit" was worth five hundred educated ministers. This new awakening of love and devotion revitalized religious, social, and political activities. The revivalist's social idealism spurred him on to reform the drunkard, free the slaves, elevate womanhood, and banish poverty and vice from the country. He used revivalistic techniques and songs to draw the attention of the masses to these problems.

Chicano Soul

Chicanos have also contributed to the soul music literature. Chicanos living in New Mexico and Southern Colorado sing their *alabados,* soulful hymns in the vernacular in praise of the Holy Sacrament. These hymns have been part of the services of the flagellant brothers. Their processions are almost identical with the processions of Spanish penitents in the 17th, 18th, and 19th centuries.[16]

Typically, the Chicano village in which *alabados* are performed has a *morada* (chapter house) of the flagellants located a short distance from the village. It is a rectangular building with two or three large rooms. One of the rooms is the oratory, housing an altar with an image of Jesus, the Virgin, and other saints. Only part of the *morada* is accessible to non-flagellants who may enter during semi-public acts of devotion. During the Lenten season the flagellants process from the *morada* to follow the stations of the cross. During this procession they may engage in whippings and sing *alabados*. In the nearby village the singing of the *ala-bados* is a profession or vocation of village minstrels. Usually two of these minstrels sing the solo part of the *alabado;* the remainder of the male members of the society join in at the chorus. The ornate melodies are highly exciting. Their texts, like ballads, often contain many stanzas.

The *alabado* "Dividido el corazon" ("Divided Heart") is a good example. Its 27 stanzas describe the suffering of the Virgin during the Passion of Christ as sung during the procession on Good Friday.[17] It begins like a ballad (romance) and ends like a *Seelenmusik* prayer. The first stanza follows:[18]

Her heart divided,
Mary cries without consolation.
She passed the night in vigilance,
meditating on the Passion.

These words are sung to a highly ornamented melody which is compressed into a narrow range like the first line of the soulful Amish version of "Wachet auf."

A Catharsis of Soul

These examples of white soulful music involve music's capacity to transport man beyond his physical environment. This, however, is not their uniqueness. Unique in these musical experiences is the exploitation of this transcendence for a sense of spiritual community and security away from a hostile world for people who felt a deep sense of alienation from the mainstream of society and especially from the established church. Finding themselves outside of the limits of mainline religious movements, they tended to develop religious expressions, liturgies, services, and songs through which they could feel secure. Their various musical expressions provided security through the Aristotelian type of *catharsis,* or ecstasy, in which music can arouse feelings of human identity and belonging —what pietistic Lutherans in the 17th century called *Seelenmusik* and what today's blacks call "soul." The reality of soul music knows no limits of race or time.

6

American Popular Music and the Blacks

In the 1960s black rhythms, black improvisational practices, and black concepts of sound energy and volume appeared in the music of the American church in the forms of folk, jazz, rock music set to worship services (masses), and hymns. All these as well as current pop songs, the way we use instruments in our pop bands and orchestras, and the distinctive quality of our American popular music, can be traced to the musical genius that came to America from Africa.

The influence of black music on American popular music has run along two lines. One channel can be traced from the plantation song to the minstrel show, to ragtime, and finally to jazz. All along this line the original black source has undergone modifications. Some modifications have come about through the requirements of popular stage and commercial enterprises as well as through technical considerations that involve instruments and recording techniques. Some changes resulted from activities of white musicians and composers. The source, however, is unmistakably black.

A second line of influence runs from the West African call-and-response chant to the American black work songs and "field hollers," to the spiritual, with all its effect on the development of the blues, to gospel singing, and finally to the rock 'n roll of the 1950s and the rock of the 1960s and 1970s.

The Minstrel Show

Throughout the greater part of the 19th century black-faced minstrels dominated the American musical theater. In their racist songs and dances minstrels aped the music and movements of the plantation blacks. Though greatly altered and modified by white imitators, the jubilee songs of the slaves were reflected in the pieces of such white minstrels as George Washington Dixon, "Daddy" Rice, and Dan Emmet. Rice made his success as a minstrel when he decided to impersonate the stable groom's song on the stage. Many other blacks contributed songs in this way to the black-faced minstrel show, which represented the first wave of music that flowed out of the black community into the mainstream of white American musical life.

Ragtime

Ragtime is the black culture's first great, memorable contribution to popular virtuoso piano music. Scott Joplin's "Maple Leaf Rag" (1899) became classic ragtime's most lasting popular hit. Classic ragtime became immortalized in the piano rags of Scott Joplin (1868-1917), James Scott (1866-1938), and the white student of Joplin, Joseph Lamb (1887-1960) and their immediate followers. Gradually its high standards of quality and form were diluted by the whites. Through the media of player-pianos, calliopes, dance bands, and commercial interests such as New York's Tin Pan Alley, this pseudo-ragtime flooded the country and became the rage for almost twenty years. John Philip Sousa made band arrangements of cakewalks, marches, and ragtime pieces and played them here and in Europe to help the cause of this "distinctly American" music.

At the turn of the century black musicians of the North were not aware of any "purer" black culture than the diluted ragtime that existed there. The playing of American and European popular songs by black syncopated orchestras was all done in the "raggy" style that conformed to the dominant tastes of the day. However, these musicians, through their connection with the "blue" tones of the black church, brought a distinctive black style into their "syncopated" music. Typical of the black dance orchestras thriving in the North at this time were James Reese Europe's various Clef Club and Tempo Club orchestras. As accompanist for the famed white dance team of Vernon and Irene Castle, Europe's Society Orchestra was largely responsible for introducing the castle walk and the fox trot to the American public.

The Blues

The blues emerge in relation to the peculiar social, cultural, economic, and emotional experience of blacks in America. As a result, the materials of the blues have not generally been available to white Americans. The classic blues singers, however, have brought their music close to white America without sacrificing its integrity. In the second decade of the century W. C. Handy popularized the blues for a great many Americans with his publication of various "blues compositions." In

1912 Handy's "Memphis Blues" appeared, followed in 1914 by his "St. Louis Blues." The decline of the ragtime craze in the middle 'teens, was followed by a "blues craze" in which Handy's compositions played an important part. Everyone began to sing the blues and all song writers began to write the blues. The orchestras of Paul Whiteman, Wilbur Sweatman, and Jim Europe all played Handy's compositions with success. But the music which resulted from this craze had little, if anything, to do with legitimate blues, because the blues could not be legitimately produced except as the expression of a peculiar culture. For this reason, the blues, in their most moving manifestations, have remained obscure to the mainstream of American culture and church music.

Jazz

By the 1920s jazz, for most Americans, meant one of two things: to the "hip" it meant the Original Dixieland Jazz band; to the "square" it meant Paul Whiteman's Orchestra. The former group had learned to imitate the turn-of-the-century black musicians of New Orleans, particularly King Oliver's Creole Band. In the second decade the Original Dixieland group moved to Chicago and in 1917 became the first jazz band to make a record, the famous "Tiger Rag." Large numbers of black groups playing in the New Orleans style did not record until the twenties when King Oliver's Creole Band cut "Dippermouth Blues" in 1923. During the 1920s serious young white musicians like Bix Beiderbecke formed styles of their own based on the Original Dixielanders' imitations of the New Orleans black music. Subsequently, great masses of imitative jazz materials began to be recorded by white musicians and were heard by large segments of white American society. Commercial radio stations from the 1920s further contributed to the spread of the white dilution of authentic jazz styles.

For the first time white Americans successfully imitated something of the legitimate feeling of Afro-American music. Jazz enabled whites to make new and valid emotional expressions based on an older Afro-American music, but which were clearly not a part of it. Jazz allowed white church musicians, here and abroad, to find new media for the syncretization of "secular" and "sacred" materials for the purposes of non-racist worship music.

The blatant, often outrageous, character of New Orleans jazz and that of its white imitators shocked the sensibilities of white genteel America. Jazz to this segment of society meant Paul Whiteman's orchestra. By 1920 Whiteman was heralded as "The King of Jazz." His numerous concert hall displays with a complete European-style orchestra catapulted jazz into the mainstream of popular music. Indeed, the appearance of the pseudo- or symphonic-jazz of Whiteman and of other dance band leaders in the entertainment world was a sure sign of the impact of jazz in America.

The expressive big bands which blacks developed between 1925 and 1935 showed that jazz could absorb new foreign elements without losing its identity, that it was, in fact, capable of evolution. This music combined older Afro-American elements with greater amounts of European tradition. Duke Ellington's sophistication, exemplified by his "Black and Tan Fantasy" of 1928, was largely the result of his ability to integrate the older blues tradition with the "whiter" styles of big-band music. By the mid-1930s this music, called "swing," found a place in the main culture. The big black bands of the late 1930s, exemplified by Count Basie's "One O'Clock Jump," played many white clubs across the country and moved deep into the mainstream. Soon white swing bands developed and played in imitation of the black bands. Since discriminatory practices made it difficult for black bands to get the same exposure to the mass audience, the national diffusion of swing was left to white leaders, such as Benny Goodman, Tommy Dorsey, Artie Shaw, and Glenn Miller.

Swing

In the 1940s swing had become an integral part of American culture. In fact, it dominated the field of popular dance and entertainment music. Swing radio programs reached the whole country, and the most popular swing musicians had their own radio shows. Swing, however, tended to submerge the more impressive acquisitions from the Afro-American musical tradition beneath a mass of "popular" commercialism.

With even more drastic dilutions of the swing style in the mid-1940s, American popular music became almost calcified. The source for a new revitalization proved to be the contemporary urban blues of the black population, a music that was called "rhythm and blues" and was distinguished by its use of electric guitars as accompanying instruments. The recording of "I can't be satisfied" by Muddy Waters in 1948 is a significant outgrowth of this style. In the 1940s the diluted versions of rhythm and blues by white singers produced a growing interest among white audiences for the authentic model, which was a synthesis of blues vocalization, jazz improvisation, and church-connected gospel singing in the black community. America came to experience "the real thing" in such recordings as "Move up a little higher" by gospel singer Mahalia

Jackson and "Baby, let me hold your hand" by blues singer Ray Charles.

Rock 'n Roll

The new popular music of the 1950s, called "rock 'n roll," combined this black rhythm and blues with elements of white country music and became personified on a national scale in the singing, playing, and gyrating of white performer Elvis Presley, particularly with such hits as "Heartbreak Hotel" and "Sh-Boom." To be sure, rock 'n roll was a flagrant commercialization of rhythm and blues. Nevertheless, it maintained an intrinsic and vital interest because its materials, particularly the "vulgar" black urban blues of the 1940s, were sufficiently alien to the general middle-class American culture. For this reason, rock 'n roll did not become as emotionally meaningless as commercial swing. It was still raw enough to stand the dilutions and in some cases even to be enhanced by its commercialization. Even its alienation from the middle class remained conspicuous, since it was often used to characterize white adolescents as "youthful offenders." Rock 'n roll was the blues form for that class of Americans that either lacked the "sophistication" of the middle-brow, or were too "naive" to get into the mainstream of American taste.

By the mid-1960s the intersection of these folk styles, black and white, had completely transformed American popular music. The popular music of the decade came to be called simply "rock," an electrified and amplified music that was unsentimental, useful in psychedelic "happenings," and exemplified by such Motown groups as "The Supremes" (female) and "The Temptations" (male). The rock style produced by these two black groups of the 1960s belongs to what is called "the Detroit sound" and comes closer than any other to being the music of another emerging middle class. Engineered by Barry Gordy for the massive teenage audience, black and white, the Detroit sound is a soft-spoken, refined, and polished soul music, which offers the appeal of popular music without compromising the strength of black elements in music. The 1964 recording hit by the Supremes, "Where did our love go?" exemplifies this creation of a broad market for a black-music product.

The rock revolution continues to dominate the popular musical expression in America. Black Americans have provided still another musical wave that has transformed the mainstream of American music.

Black Music and White Musicians

In his book, *Urban Blues,* Charles Keil states that blacks did not impose their values on white Americans via song and dance; rather, their song and dance were appropriated by white Americans via the white-controlled music business, music publishers, record companies, and radio stations. For example, Benny Goodman rose to fame on Fletcher Henderson's big-band arrangements. Elvis Presley derived his style from the black rhythm-and-blues performers of the late 1940s. Peggy Lee imitates many of Ray Charles' most popular songs. The black innovators have generally resented this pattern and have responded to each appropriation by re-expressing American black identity and attitude in a new and revitalized way. Each successive commercialization of a black style by white Americans has stimulated the black community and its musical spokesmen to generate a new music that is a new black property. This appropriation-revitalization process has therefore largely determined the present state of American popular music.

Since the days of the first recordings and especially during the last two decades, black music has become progressively "reactionary," that is, more African in its essentials and more consistent with the various jazz and blues styles in their initial phases. These are the symbolic referents of in-group solidarity for the black masses and the more intellectual segments of the black bourgeoisie. Black jazzmen have fallen back on the blues, bluesmen have inserted into their playing more elements from the black church, and black drummers have worked toward the crossed-triplet rhythms of West Africa. Afro-Cuban rhythms have grown increasingly important in jazz during the last twenty years, and in rhythm and blues in more recent times. Many records that grew out of the dance craze known as the Watusi had an Afro-Cuban flavor.

Consequently, year by year American popular music has come to sound more and more like African popular music. The rhythmic complexity and subtlety, the emphasis on percussive sound qualities, the call-and-response pattern, the characteristic vocal elements (shout, growl, falsetto), blues chromaticism, blues and gospel chord progressions, black vocabulary, and Afro-American dance steps are some of the traits Keil cites as having become increasingly prominent in American popular music.

Also, white copies of black originals have come to show greater skill, sensitivity, and fidelity than ever before. On the "big-beat" radio stations it is increasingly difficult to separate white and black performers, largely because many black stylists have eliminated some of the coarser qualities from the blues and gospel styles, while a number of white performers have perfected their handling of black vocal accent, inflection patterns, and phrasing. The success of "The Rolling Stones," for example, in their recordings of "Satisfied" and "Backstreet Girl" is largely because they took the style of the black man's blues, country or city, and combined it with the visual image of white American non-conformity.

The ever-expanding white audience has been so well conditioned by forty years or more of successive appropriations that the latest black style is no longer considered dangerous or controversial, but is eagerly swallowed up in its original or slightly diluted form.

It is not surprising therefore that black music as discussed in the preceding and following chapters has found its way into the worship music of the church. The demand for church music that is derived from the black culture, whether in folk, jazz, pop, or rock styles, usually by the younger generation, seems to indicate a deficiency of some sort in the American church-music mainstream.

Just as the church's clinging to exclusively traditional music was a symptom of losing touch with the real world of today, so the adoption of black-derived musical expression is part of the church's struggle to overcome its deficiency, to capture the attention of people in today's culture, and to prove its relevance. The church is beginning to face the fact that today's church member lives in a musical culture largely dependent on the creative drive of black musicians. Thus the move toward black-derived church music is a move toward reality.

7

Folk, Jazz, Pop, and Rock Masses

Twentieth-century man, like any other man, is much involved in his musical culture, but it is not the culture of the concert hall or the church. His music is the music of the media, the popular, mass-produced music that bombards him at work, in his living room, in restaurants, at the theaters, and even in his car on the way to work in the morning.

As a result, American composers have turned their attention to popular music based on black music origins in their effort to create a new and relevant church music. Many have looked to the rich resources of American popular music, from jazz to rock, from folk to Muzak, for musical materials from which to create music that can arouse feelings of identity and belonging. The variety of attempts is astounding: jazz masses, pop masses, rock masses, folk masses, rock opera, folk services, jazz services. What is exciting about the new American music is its roots in popular music derived from the black culture.

Black Materials: African Devices

To assess the impact of black music on American church music we look first at masses created in Africa that use African devices. The best known settings of the mass using African devices are the *Missa Luba* and the *Missa Bantu*. Both are missionary masses in that white missionaries were responsible for the final arrangement of the mass and the organization and directing of the black choirs—in the *Luba* mass, a boys' and teachers' choir; in the *Bantu* mass, a women's choir. Both masses had a great impact on the development of succeeding masses. The *Luba* mass particularly influenced many Latin American masses, specifically the *Misa Criolla* by the Argentinian, Ariel Ramirez.

The various parts of the *Missa Luba* are based on Congolese tunes. The Kyrie, Gloria, and Credo are based on music of the *Kasala* from Nganganjika (Kasai). The Hosanna uses an authentic dance rhythm of the Kasai, while the Agnus Dei uses a song of *Becca Luba*. In addition to the African sounds, white listeners will discover Afro-Cuban sonorities in the joyfulness that permeates the entire work, in the maraca-like sounds at the beginning of the Gloria and Agnus Dei, and in the marimba-like sounds in the Credo. The African element of improvisation can be heard in the beautiful, melismatic handling of the word "crucifixus" in the Credo. The drumbeats of Africa accompany chants and choral settings of the entire mass. Actually the chant is enhanced by the percussive ostinati. Some western sounds of a "black Obernkirchen choir," so to speak, occur in the Sanctus with its third progressions. There is also a reminder of the sweet Roman Catholic mass music written by California mission composers of the 19th century, such as Father Sixto Durán in his *Missa De Angelis*. This western sound is abruptly contrasted by the wild "cha-cha-cha" rhythms of the Hosanna. The *Luba* mass sets a precedent for many other masses by combining various ingredients, in this case, of African, Afro-Cuban, and western music.

The *Missa Bantu* is full of Africanisms of a more varied nature. There is, of course, the perpetual drumbeat in many different patterns. Antiphonal singing is assisted by a great deal of imitative singing. Sometimes it is coupled with characteristic African drone effects. Typical African parallelisms of fifths extend to three-part harmony. The high-pitched soprano parts with which the Kyrie begins remind us of Killmayer's Kyrie, a composition by a contemporary German composer that transmits a feeling of *ecstasis*, of "soul." This *Bantu* mass is full of such ecstatic quality. It seems to be driven by this quality in the music for the words "qui tollis peccata mundi" of the Gloria. Since all sections of the mass Propers involve organ and western chant, and all parts of the Ordinary involve percussion instruments and the choir of the black nuns, the mass effectively combines western and African elements.

Black Materials: Rhythm and Harmony

The influence of black music on jazz, folk, pop, and rock music has tended to overcome the dominance of the melody by emphasizing vital and energetic rhythm, the rich shadings of non-white "worried" intervals and harmonic colors, and the modern art of polyrhythmic counterpoint. Harmonic procedures such as the use of the ninth chord, added sixth chords, parallel chord progressions, and the standard blues chord give the prelude and the anthem of Summerlin's *Requiem for Mary Jo* its flavor of predictable unpredictability. In Kent Schneider's *Celebration for Modern Man* the alternation between minor seventh chords

93

every two beats with e minor seventh chords for eight measures, followed by a middle section of e flat minor seventh chords and f minor seventh chords for another eight bars, followed by a repetition of the first eight bars, gives an effect of freedom and tension within very narrow limits.

Black Materials: Improvisation

The art of improvisation and variation, a gift of the black culture, has added another dimension to jazz, folk, pop, and rock masses. Actually improvisation is no newcomer to American church music. Shortages of funds and limitations of personnel have often forced church musicians and school music teachers to find alternatives. Choirs are often unable to sing the music as it is written. Cuts have to be made on the spot; Lowell Mason, the practical teacher-composer-businessman, saw this problem and provided many arrangements of classical European music so that relatively unskilled American church choirs could sing them. Even today, we rarely hear Handel's *Messiah* as it was originally composed, and we almost never hear Dubois' *Seven Last Words* to the sounds of a symphony orchestra.

This history of changing music to adjust to a particular situation makes the step to actual improvisation in church music a relatively short one. Unhampered by written-out scores, black musicians in Africa and in the Americas have developed a sophisticated art of improvisation and variation. Since 20th century church music uses black materials, many of the new creations reveal extensive use of improvisation.

John Gensel and the Joe Newman Quintet in a recording of *O Sing to the Lord a New Song* achieve an effective synthesis of Michael Praetorius' *variation per choros* technique (presenting a given chorale melody by alternating ensembles) with the jazz improvisation principle. In the improvisation of Psalm 150, improvisation No. 1 is given to the trumpet, No. 2 is given to the guitar and piano solo, No. 3 to the piano and trumpet, No. 4 to the bowed string bass, No. 5 to the cymbal, and No. 6 to the trumpet and piano. While Gensel and the Joe Newman Quintet make improvisation a core part of the vesper service, Richard Koehneke uses improvisation only in the postlude to a very modern setting of the Lutheran liturgy. Summerlin's many jazz settings make abundant use of improvisation. In his score for the *Liturgy of the Holy Spirit* the tenor is asked to improvise a melody to the words, "Majestic mystery of human life, of man and woman made in God's image." Later the soprano is asked to improvise to the words, "In silence and alone we speak your name."

Planned improvisation occurs when the clarinet and bass part improvise after "Hundred-twentieth St., the alcoholic leans against its bricks" and at the end, "And then of a sudden I saw a star," and when the secular text about life in New York's streets is abruptly changed to "sudden darkness, there were no street lights. Good God! there's a sky. . . . And of a sudden, there was a star."

In his *Theme for Grace* Guaraldi has written controlled and restrained piano improvisations for the communion service of the Episcopal church. The piano functions more as a soloist than does the organ in a traditional church service. This solo function of the piano is evident when the piano accompanies the congregational or choral parts, not only by doubling the melody as an organ would sometimes do, but also by elaborating with its jazzy counter-punctuations to produce a delicate polyrhythmic effect. Sometimes pianistic figures such as tremoli, rolls, and arpeggios are used. This kind of piano-led service, with many improvisational high points, creates the impression of a graceful, well-behaved way of adding glamour and etiquette to a well-structured ritual. In this kind of a service there are no ecstatic outcries of the "soul." Everything, including the piano improvisations, follows protocol.

Black Materials: The Black Spiritual

Some North American pop masses use the black spiritual. In Bruce Prince-Joseph's short missa, "The Whole World in His Hands," the spiritual with its text serves as the center of the entire service. In spite of the omnipresence of the spiritual, in spite of the jazz sounds, syncopations, and polyrhythms, a traditional church sound predominates. This is not a spontaneous, exhilarating jazz service. Rather it is a festival Sunday service by a rich white church on New York's Fifth Avenue in which the sounds and rhythms of jazz music are added to the basic sounds of traditional solo, choral, and organ music. The element of Fifth Avenue church music is particularly evident in the simulated chaotic presentations of the Sanctus. Thus it is a token spiritual mass, created by whites, who have borrowed black materials without understanding their meaning and spirit.

Black Materials in Summerlin and Tirro

Jazz and church music are merged in classical fashion in the works of Ed Summerlin, Frank Tirro, Dave Brubeck, and Leonard Bernstein. In Summerlin's *Liturgy of the Holy Spirit*, to the text of the late William Robert Miller, jazz harmonies prevail completely over white harmonies. Only the short hymn, "O loving Father, we turn to you," is without blues harmonization. Instead, a recurrent ostinato bass theme is stated ten times. In all other sections jazz makes itself felt through the colorful harmonizations of melodic segments often based on a gap-scale pattern. This occurs in the hymn, "How sweet and holy is the Word," the chorus section to "O myst'ry greatest all of love eternal," the climactic section, "O mystery tremendous," and the recessional hymn, "And now we go our varied ways," in which a simple melody is harmonized in a jazzy manner. A typical black device, that of constant exchange of vocal to instrumental, instrumental to vocal writing is used extensively in the beginning of the work.

Summerlin also uses jazz inspirations in his *The Coming of Christ,* Parousia, Part III, in which he develops the entire movement out of an initial blues figure.

Frank P. Tirro's *American Jazz Mass* effectively combines SATB choral writing with an instrumental ensemble of trumpet, alto, baritone sax, string bass, and drums. Frequent ostinato patterns help to structure the various mass movements. In the Credo, ostinato pattern I and its variants accompany the words, "I believe in one God . . . came down from heaven," pattern II in combination with pattern Ia and a variant of pattern II extends from the words "and was crucified" to the words "whose kingdom shall have no end."

Black Materials in Brubeck and Bernstein

In Summerlin's and Tirro's compositions black melodies, harmonies, rhythms, bass patterns, and choice of instruments prevail over classical musical forms. In

Brubeck's and Bernstein's works, however, the opposite holds true. In *The Light in the Wilderness* Brubeck —a newcomer to the field of church music—successfully combines the 19th century Anglo-American oratorio with his own jazz idiom. The choral and solo atmosphere of works such as American Horatio Parker's *Hora Novissima* hovers over Brubeck's frequently alternating 3/4, 4/4, and 5/4 measures, over the delightfully syncopated and polyrhythmic comments of "The great commandment" (No. VI), over the folksy "Let not your heart be troubled," into the rather overstated and pompous final "Praise" chorus. The sounds of the traditional Anglo-American oratorio from the turn of the century—a tradition still very much alive in this country—tend, unfortunately, to dominate Brubeck's fresh and swinging piano improvisations. Sometimes these improvisations occur as chorale variations, after the chorus has sung its part, sometimes as an obligato part of the choral numbers. One of them echoes "The Duke," one of Brubeck's best jazz compositions.

In Bernstein's *Mass* no single style prevails over all others; jazz is only one of many styles Bernstein uses to create a collage suggesting contemporary man's struggle for identification and redemption. The *Mass* combines amplified rock sound orchestrations of Shostakovich, Poulenc, Kostelanetz, Orff, and Stravinsky, and the melodies of Beethoven. Bernstein also draws inspiration from the sound of the Swingle Singers, Broadway, from his own *West Side Story*, American marching bands, from college madrigal groups, and jazz.

Through the many different sounds, motions, lights, and colors called for in the score of this *Mass*, Bernstein communicates well with the common person of our time, generally glued to the TV, to contemporary man whose new "tribalism" is strongly supported by multi-media experience.

Since no one style either in classical music or in popular music can claim predominance today, contemporary man naturally seems to ask for polystylism. Musical mixed marriages are the call of the day. Bernstein has made an ambitious attempt at multiplicity, polystylism, and mixed marriages of the arts.

There is enthusiasm, freshness, and naturalness in Bernstein's religious show music. Numbers like "God said: let there be light" (No. IX) could be taken out of context and would make sense like any single hit tune from any of his other musicals. His Credo (No. X) has the simple structure of a good production number of any Broadway musical. The element of the show dance is more important than the liturgical content. Who has ever heard of an Agnus Dei march? *West Side Story's* high-heeled sharks and their women dancing wildly at the gym, on the streets, and on the rooftops are reincarnated as a dance around the sacramental objects. And yet a serene church-choir sound emerges when needed. In the recessional "Almighty Father" (end of No. XVII), after the destruction of the order of the mass and the vessels of communion and the subsequent silence, Bernstein finds the spark of true choral church music sung by *all* voices, including the stage instrumentalists. He told the *Time* reporter-researcher Rosemarie Tauris Zadakov:

> Everyone in that silence has to look inside himself, and find in himself that spark of God. Not in any icon or symbol or trappings of religion but inside. Only when he finds that can he begin to relate to another person, then to a group, ultimately to society. And this is the miracle I saw take place; the waves of tenderness, these waves

of touching and embracing, began to spread from the stage to the house, until they passed through the whole audience and then even into the street. I saw people embracing strangers on the streets— cops, just ordinary people.

Bernstein takes a stand in favor of worship with total involvement as practiced in the black churches of this country: ecstasy, emotionalism, spontaneity, and community emphasis emerge from this mixed-marriage, black-white service of Judeo-Christian origin.

Black Materials in Jesus Christ Superstar

As Bernstein's *Mass* favors an involvement in the totality of sound, so does the rock opera *Jesus Christ Superstar*. It is unthinkable without the influence of black music. The creation of Andrew Lloyd Webber and Tim Rice, it had its first public performance in October, 1970. The music, while basically streamlined flawless rock, is tinted significantly by qualities of black music. This black element is especially noticeable in the music of Judas and Jesus, whose parts call for ad-lib ornamentation and use of the falsetto range. Black-originated call-and-response patterns create a hectic effect when Judas asks in the opening scene, "What's the buzz?" The commenting two-part chorus responds, articulating a strong rhythmic pattern with virtually no tune. Herod's song has elements of black-created ragtime. The style of the black spiritual appears when the chorus chants, "Well done, Judas, good old Judas" and later, "Poor old Judas, so long Judas," and a touch of sensual Calypso humanizes Mary Magdalene's song of love "Try not to get worried." Ostinato bass patterns characteristic of Afro-American music and of rock are spread throughout the entire opera.

Other Materials: The March

Popular masses of today often employ the march, a basic form of group music making. Its use lends qualities of strength, vigor, faith, and conviction. Clarence Jo Rivers' first jazz mass of the triptych *A Mass Dedicated to the Brotherhood of Man* is unique in that the entire work is a jazz march mass. The Kyrie and the Agnus Dei are slow, and the Gloria and the Sanctus are fast marches. In Summerlin's *Requiem for Mary Jo* a black "Onward Christian Soldiers" beat permeates the entire worship service. This beat is strictly enforced, even in the jazz improvisations of the first congregational hymn. The second version (adult choir and piano accompaniment) of the *Missa Apalachia* contains tunes provided with an oom-ta-ta piano accompaniment that resembles the march beat sounds of simple country bands. Guitar masses like Ray Repp's *Mass* and *Second Mass for Young Americans* employ the beat of guitar-bass to accompany youth singing marching songs in the name of a rediscovered Christ. The Nicene Creed March of Ian Mitchell's *The American Folk Song Mass* provides a remarkable example of church music reflecting the youthfulness of the church.

Other Materials: Occasional Use of Folk Songs

In a letter to Lord Kames of Edinburgh, Benjamin Franklin described an ideal of natural music that fits many new *folk hymns* of today. Franklin advocated a music in which the melody rules over harmony and rhythm. His aesthetic ideal of simple tune-making was perpetuated in the appealing parlor songs of Stephen Foster and William Russell of the 19th century and in the tunes of Lowell Mason, often imitated by innumerable church-tune composers of the 19th and 20th

101

centuries. Without exception these tunes were harmonized simplistically.

Although many of the new *folk hymns* belong to this Franklin-Foster-Mason lineage of rustic, folksy writing, very few *folk masses* apply this technique. An example of folk harmonization can be seen in Father Rivers' *A Mass Dedicated to the Brotherhood of Man* and *Mass for World Peace*. The simple folk harmonies of these masses are appealing, and harmonic interaction of voices enables singers and listeners to believe in the possibilities of harmony, love, warmth, and understanding among men. *The Mass for World Peace,* however, offers a simplistic, unacceptable sample. Its first six numbers are hymn-songs full of cliché-ridden guitar patterns that create an illusion of folk sounds.

Other Materials: The Dance

Popular dance and song, together with the sound of black-influenced rhythms and instruments, occur most frequently in Latin American compositions for the church. In ten of twelve numbers in J. Tolaba's and H. E. Lobos' *El Evangelio Criollo* (The Creole Gospel) —an oratorio of the life, death, and resurrection of Christ—the rhythms of the Argentinian dances, the *bailecito, carnavalito, chamaca, chacerera, canción, chaya, cueca, estilo* and *milonga,* are used. In his *Misa Criolla,* the Argentinian Ariel Ramirez used the rhythm of the *vidala-baguala* (Northern Argentina) in the Kyrie, of the *carnavalito* (North) for the Gloria, of the *chacarera trunca* (Central Argentina) for the Credo, of the Bolivian *carnaval cochabambino* for the Sanctus, and the *estilo pampea-ano* is the basis of the Agnus Dei.

Vicente Bianchi in his *Missa a la Chilena* for all five sections of the Ordinary of the Mass employed the rhythms of the central region of Chile. The Kyrie is written in the style of the Araucanos, the fierce original inhabitants of Chile, the Gloria represented by the rhythm of the *refalosa,* the Credo by a *tonada;* the Sanctus uses the form of the simple *cancion chilena;* the Agnus Dei is written on the rhythm of the *trote nortino;* whereas the most typical song-dance form of Chile, the *cueca,* is reserved for the additional Alleluia finale. The Agnus Dei is used as the Agnus Dei of the *Missa Panamericana.*

Leclerc's *Missa Panamericana* uses the music to the processional, recessional, and the communion from two recordings by the Perales, a group of four seminarians from Chile, "Guitarras de campo y cielo" and "En carreta de arreboles"; the music to the Kyrie, from Delfino Madrigal Gil's "Missa Mexicana"; to the Gloria, from R. P. Anselvio Murrillo's "Missa Ranchera"; and to the Credo and Santo from Rafael Carrión's "Missa en Mexico." All selections are arranged to sound like a mariachi band. This work is actually a Mexican pan-American Mass. Leclerc believes that church music should be spontaneous, that it should be music *con carne* (with beef), *espina* (guts), *nervios* (nerve), that it cannot be music *bajo mando* (under command), as ordered by the church authorities. It should be church music *bajo el estado de canto* (under the condition of singing), in other words, the element of ecstasy through singing, the element of becoming totally involved, should be prevalent. The familiarity of the mariachi sound allows everybody in the church to identify themselves with the Almighty.

Other Materials: Mestizo and Indian Sounds

Black people's church music is often poor people's church music. Poor people's church music—black, red, brown or white—often uses its own native musical language. People who are not poor often write or compose church music for or about the poor. Harry V. Lojewski's *The Mariachi Mass,* is a poor man's version of the rich and full sound of the Mexican mariachi. It is a manufactured piece of American church music which contains little of the marvelous fiddling practices or the rich sounds of the brass instruments of true mariachi music. It only teases the listener's attention with the poor man's dreams of traveling to exotic places.

Quite different with much more *carne* (beef), is Jean-Marc Leclerc's *Missa Tepozteca.* This mass, written specifically for a congregation of a poor to lower-income people of Tepozteca, only 95 km. from Mexico City, uses Aztec, autochthonous, and modern instruments in addition to simple two- or three-part choral harmonies. The instruments are taken from the congregation's immediate environment or from the historical past of which they still are aware. Thus the instruments in the processional Entrada are a cow horn, then the Aztec *teponaxtli,* then the *chirimia* (a folk instrument similar to the clarinet) to the accompaniment of a snare drum. The Kyrie employs guitars, sea shells, gourds, and string bass while the Meditación is done by a banjo recitative against guitar accompaniment and the accordion. Some of the previously mentioned instruments, including the sea shells, are employed for the Sanctus, Amen of the Canon, and the Recessional. All melodies are taken from the actual repertoire of the people—the members of the congregation and the rural population.

A performance of this mass evoked various responses from the members of the congregation in attendance. For some of them it was nothing special. Others expressed strong reactions: "I did not remember the meat nor my children during the mass"; "Am I a cow that they call me with a cow horn?"; or "The signal of the horn is well in place as one heard it in the wars of liberation that they should attack more fiercely."

The Padres Oblatos de Maria Immaculata composed for their parish Nuestra Señora de la Asunción de Llallagua in Bolivia a *Misa Incáica* in the Quechua language. This work, a setting of the Ordinary and Propers of the mass is scored for the native instruments of the Bolivian Indians and *mestizos*—the *quena*, harp, hand drum, and guitar. It probably comes close to the ideal described by the Maryknoll Father Francis W. Mahoney in his writings about the incorporation of native rites with the Christian liturgy of the Aymara Church of Juli in Peru.

Dance rhythms known to Indians and *mestizos* alike appear in the Introduction, the Sanctus, Agnus Dei, and the Cántico de Despedida (Canticle of Farewell). The melodies reflect the native pentatonic melodic patterns. The sound of the instruments is fully enjoyed, each instrument being introduced as a solo and performing solo for a time. The sounds of the *quena* seem to soar to the heights of the mountains and give the flavor of Andean music. Guitar and harp music provide the foundations in the valleys. The beat of the drum bridges the valleys and mountain peaks, *quenas* and guitars and harps. The choir sings in unison or in simple thirds which sound like the popular singing in modern Inca land. The Credo contrasts the chant of the leader with its phrases in Latin and the folk refrain of the choir. A great feeling of belonging, of brotherhood among Bolivian Indians and *mestizos,* emanates from the singing of the leader and of the choir.

Reminiscences of Different Styles in Folk, Jazz, Pop, and Rock Masses

Many jazz masses apply the sound of popular music directly to the worship service. Beaumont's *20th Cen-*

tury Folk Mass with its "sound the trumpet" motif is borrowed from Harry James from the early 1940s. The musical climaxes of this work bring to mind an image of a Fred Astaire waving his hat.

John Gensel and Joe Newman's Quintet sounds like Miles Davis in his middle period. Newman's use of standard tunes, "Willow Weep for Me," and "Body and Soul," draws directly from the standard repertory of the late '50s.

Summerlin in his *Requiem for Mary Jo* used the very typical "cool" or "West Coast" octet sound of the late '50s.

Guaraldi's *Theme to Grace* with its abundance of jazz-waltz patterns reminds us of the late '50s and Steve Allen's famous "Gravy Waltz." Guaraldi also borrows the tendency toward understatement and restraint used by jazz pianists of the '50s, Ahmad Jamal and Bill Evans.

Bruce Prince-Joseph set the creed in his mass, *The Whole World in His Hands,* as a choral recitation over a persistent beat, a technique that reminds us of the beatniks of the mid-'50s reading their poetry to jazz accompaniment.

In Schneider's *Celebration for Modern Man* all of the improvised solos are very "hip" readings of modern jazz typical of the early '60s. The tenor sax plays many John Coltrane mannerisms of that time, and an overall "modal" sound, very typical of the early '60s prevails.

For the *Liturgies of This Day,* Schneider chose the "new thing" sound of the middle '60s, a kind of free-form improvisation without preset harmonic, rhythmic, or even metrical rules.

Galt MacDermod in his *Divine Hair-Mass in F* borrowed melodies from the rock musical *Hair* for the Propers of the service; Introit ("Aquarius"), Sequence

("What a piece of work is man"), Offertory ("Three-Five-Zero-Zero" and "Where do I go?"). Although MacDermod wrote original music for the Ordinary of this work, his composition never strays far from the rock idiom of *Hair*. Galt MacDermod's combinations of sound are amazing. To the cathedral sounds of high-class church music the raw, natural, exhilarant qualities of black, folk, jazz, and rock music are added. This *Divine Hair-Mass in F* seems to shatter the walls of the church nave, to throw sound energies against the highest and most hidden parts of the church building, only to have them roll back on the congregation. It seems able to carry the congregation's heartbeats to the whole world. This sound-splurge rises and falls with the exchange of two rival timbres, the electronic *(Hair* selection, Proper) and the organ (newly composed, Ordinary). Even the organ prelude, the only part of the work to use the traditional sound of the organ, fills the space of the church with warmth and energy through the application of traditional chord progressions. The organ mixes its traditional sound with the melody of Aquarius. The *Aquarius* melody becomes the *alter ego* of a Bach chorale.

From the preceding discussion it becomes evident that church music today attempts to add the new dimensions of black music to the established church music culture of a Palestrina-Bach heritage. It tries to move away, for instance, from the cliché rhythms of the isorhythmic hymn-chorale that helped to shape the standardized anthems used by most church choirs in this country. It replaces it with more varied and complex rhythmic configurations of Afro-American vintage. It affirms the diversity, vitality, and newness of the black musical experience as an essential part of America's church musical culture. It promotes the use of America's varied and rich folk and pop music.

The New Folk Hymn

The election of President Kennedy in 1960 brought to culmination a modern folk culture that had originated in the late '50s. Many students from the more liberal Northern universities as well as the non-academic intelligentsia welcomed this new culture typified by the guitar and the gentle strains of folk songs performed by heroes such as Harry Belafonte, The Weavers, and the Kingston Trio. These heroes were protagonists of a new anti-mass culture that sought new musical forms. Gradually the followers of the new folk culture rejected these first heroes for the expressions of more authentic folk people. Thus the people involved in this culture moved toward higher artistic standards and came to appreciate a different culture, one almost untouched by the advanced technology and one that was more human. Folk music demanded quiet listening and reflection. It mediated between the inarticulate rock of the '50s and the heavily articulate rock of the '60s. Among the new folk artists, Bob Dylan, whose folk hero was Woodie Guthrie, was able to break through. He, along with other young people, developed a new genre, a genre not only struggling against the bourgeoisification of popular music and culture but also against the old folk forms themselves. This new musical form represented the urban folk culture.

General Characteristics of the New Hymns

Folk hymn culture, however, has only slight connections with urban folk culture. Folk hymn culture is a mass culture, sponsored by youth and the church. Although it strives toward new concepts of church music, the goals of folk hymn culture are the same as the goals of the classical hymn culture—to praise God in a meaningful way. Folk hymns of the "now" generation, like folk culture in general, are sensitive to humanity.

By their diversity the new folk hymns tend to defy definition. They are certainly not limited to the musical style usually associated with the term "folk." Rather, their musical style is eclectic, drawing from the diverse musical vocabulary of modern urban society. Through their music and their messages modern folk hymns strive to provide a new sense of individuality, of humanity, and of wholeness in a society that seems to deny all of these things. Their texts are dedicated to this theme, although their musical expression ranges from a commercialized folk sound to modified black-inspired jazz and rock sounds, from imitations of medieval carols to the sooth phrases of Muzak. While these hymns are mostly the property of young people, the members of the "downstairs" church, they are published and sung with the general approval of the "upstairs" church.

General Sound of the New Hymns

The sound of urban folk culture's The Weavers is imitated in a few folk hymn settings. In Ray Repp's "To Be Alive," from his *Sing Praise to God,* The Weavers sound is "told to the whole population." "Isn't this a time?" from *Soulful Sounds for a Church in Change* borrows its title from a Weavers' song with the same title.

Some folk hymns have a rather introspective, sub-dued sound. The sound of the guitar, a sound that does not carry far, effectively evokes a reflective mood. Often the sound of Muzak successfully replaces the sound of the guitar. Whenever its effects are used in connection with folk hymns it may have constructive, positive results. Thus, in "One little piece of mystery" from *For Mature Adults Only* by Norman Habel and Richard Koehneke the Muzak-like type of accompaniment gives the listener a religious experience that is smooth and full of feeling. The phenomenon of music as background is perpetuated in the many background choir effects used in folk hymn settings. The socially oriented "Give me your hand" from Robert Blue's *Run, Come See* uses a coda of humming effects to evoke feelings of togetherness, belonging, and identification.

Specific Characteristics: Musical Form

Folk hymn culture has access to one of the largest musical institutions in this country, the church. Its hymns are a body of poetry and music that use strict and simple forms, such as the song, the ballad, the refrain songs, and many others.

Most of the hymns are strophic songs—the same tune is sung for all stanzas. Many strophic hymns are refrain songs consisting of an initial refrain followed

111

by a solo part. Ray Repp's "Allelu" is a well-known refrain hymn.

Some hymns are ballads, narrative songs with many stanzas. A beautiful example is "The ballad of holy history," which consists of 19 stanzas, most of which are sung to the tune of the ballad proper, while stanzas 3, 6, 10, 15 are sung to a second tune.[1]

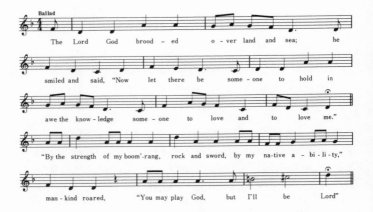

Through the use of the hexatonic scale this ballad has a certain modal flavor. Like many other folk hymns it tries to recreate the flavor of the medieval carol-ballad. By doing so it becomes a typical "antique-store" product of our time, something new and yet a product that looks like something used, worn out, of past ages. In this it is traditionally American, like the imitation Gothic church and college structures built at the turn of the century, the stained glass windows in many American churches, or the shingled roofs on houses that imitate the simple homes on the American frontier.[2] Pseudo-modal music in the style of the medieval carol draws life from an impulse similar to that which motivates young people to wear patched jeans, shorts, and coats today.

Stories of the main personalities of the Christian church have been the subject of oratorios by Handel and the famous passions by Johann Sebastian Bach. John and Amanda Ylvisaker develop musico-biographical sketches from the New Testament in *Follow Me*. They consider it a book, full of stories, worth telling in a new musical language—folk, jazz, pop, and rock combined.

Specific Characteristics: Musical Figures

Baroque church composers used special musical figures to significant words in cantatas or oratorios. Heinrich Schütz[3] and Johann Sebastian Bach[4] have left us many famous examples of Figurenmusik.

Modern folk-hymn troubadours use a similar technique. In the modern folk-hymn tradition, Paul Quinlan in the recorded version of his Psalm 114 gives figural treatment to the word "tremble." In the recorded version of his "Raindrops" Robert Blue sets "raindrops" dripping in his guitar introduction.

Specific Characteristics: March, Dance, and Rock

Some of the new folk hymns are march hymns. "Clap your hands" is a straightforward, almost monomotivic refrain march hymn by Ray Repp, written in the original key of "A mighty fortress is our God," C major (Ionian).

113

Other folk hymns borrow melodies and harmonizations from the black-originated blues. Here is a magnificent example of Ed Summerlin's "Shared Bread": [5]

Bread   of   bread   as   life   of   life,

bread   to   eat   with   strength   to   give.____   Bread   from

field   and   mill   and   store;   Bread   to   nour - ish,

life __ to   live.   Bread!   Bread!   Bread!

Another type of folk-hymn melody calls specifically for a rock beat accompaniment. It is Ed Summerlin's "Hello! and did you hear the word." [6]

Paul Quinlan's folk-rock psalms have new music for each strophe of the text. Many folk hymns involve responsorial or antiphonal singing in which the hymn is shared between men's and women's voices as it occurs in "With joyful lips," or between a soloist and chorus as in Sister Germaine's songs. The American lining-out practice is revived in "The witness song" from Blue's *Run, Come See*. Here the choir repeats literally what the soloist has sung first. Since these literal repetitions are done at a fast pace, the tune gains in zip, drive, youthfulness.

Folk hymn performers and composer/arrangers do not shy away from specific dance patterns. They use these nostalgic materials with the belief that familiar forms communicate better than patterns which have not been tested in the history of popular music. Thus we encounter the waltz beat in Paul Quinlan's Psalm 15, "Who will dwell," and in his Psalm 24, "Praise the holy of holies." "Yes, Amen" from Blues *Run, Come See* is a genuine "Amen polka." The beat of the *bolero* appears in John and Amanda Ylvisaker's "The Night Was Cold." The calypso beat is present in "Zacchaeus" of *Joy Is Like the Rain*. Some folk hymns specify modern amplification devices such as echo chambers. Through a moderate sound of black-connected rock, jazz, and pop instrumentation and electrification, the composers/arrangers hope to make the message of the text more honest, more pressing, more contemporary. This sound is applied to the strophic song forms, the ballads, the refrain hymns, and the responsorial singing in order to make it more palatable and bring it closer to the staged, prepared, managed, manicured sound of America's adolescents.

Specific Characteristics: Borrowing

One of the most common ways of writing new folk hymns is not to write them at all but to borrow well-known tunes of the past and present, of both sacred and secular origin. This procedure the church has used with great success in its long history of hymn production. It is known as *contrafacta* technique. The editors of *Songs for Today* use the first phrase of the venerable German Easter *Leise* from the 12th century, "Christ ist erstanden" for the text of Psalm 23, "The Lord is my shepherd." [7]

In Carlton R. Young's *Songbook for Saints and Sinners* John Ylvisaker borrows the leading motif of "Joy to the world" for his version of the doxology, "Thanks be to God." [8] Numerous are the examples in which well-known black spirituals, melodies from Nigeria, Thailand, West Indies, South Africa, and many European countries are provided with new texts. Sometimes the borrowing is adequate, sometimes it is tasteless.

One example of poor taste is to use the melody of the vigorous chanty, "What shall we do with a drunken sailor?" for the text entitled "Jonah." [9]

Specific Characteristics: New Texts for Old Ones

The early Christian church added, inserted, and supplemented new texts for old ones. Notable examples include the *stichera* of the Syrian chant, the *odes* of the Byzantine chant, and the *tropes* of the medieval Roman church. Robert Blue in his *Run, Come See* chooses a completely free, ode-like treatment for his Magnificat ballad. A trope-like structure is used in "Christ Light" of the same collection. The hymn begins with the well-known text "The Lord is my light and my salvation" only to continue in a free fashion. Paul Quinlan's many rock psalms are free paraphrases of the old psalm texts. They clarify 20th-century man's relationship with God. His folk-rock psalm arrangements are not abrasive or incendiary in sound. His "The Lord is my shepherd" (Psalm 23) is a controlled tune of moderate speed. It sounds like an old love song. His "Come, let us sing" (Psalm 95) is dependable in its atmosphere of *Gemütlichkeit*. His "Glory to God" (Psalm 122) is a controlled rock march. His "Glory to the Father" (Psalm 92) is a nostalgic psalm polka.

Publishing the New Hymns

Folk hymns have come into existence with the influence of the church. These hymns are filled with characteristic expressions of religious feelings, dreams, and goals of young people within the structure of the church. *Twelve Folksongs and Spirituals,* compiled and arranged by David N. Johnson, was published by Augsburg Publishing House in 1968. *Hymns for Now (I, II, III)* were published by Concordia Publishing House in 1967, 1970, and 1972 as issues of the *Workers Quarterly* (I) and of *Resources for Youth Ministry* (II, III) respectively. *Risk,* Vol. II, *New Hymns for a New Day,* was published by the Youth Department of the World Council of Churches, Geneva, 1966. *Songs for Celebration* was published by Kent Schneider in 1969 for The Center for Contemporary Celebration.

Most of the hymns are printed in books of different sizes for various performance possibilities: for unison, guitar and chorus, mixed voices with flute or guitar accompaniment, mixed voices in the format of the traditional American Protestant hymn book, for women's voices and accompaniment, and others. Most of the books include an introduction that discusses the appropriateness of the materials selected and operate with conservative and utilitarian principles to recommend their use. Such introductions state that the "forms are intended to supplement those already in use." [10] They include "songs . . . found in the emerging church as it celebrates and represents the good news." [11] They say: "We offer this collection to stimulate, to provoke, to explore, to enrich Christian singing. . . . If in time you want to discard what we have assembled in favor of something else which speaks more fully to modern life as you know it, we will feel this booklet has been a complete success." [12]

Another collection begins: "This issue of *Risk* is a recipe book, meaning not to be imitated but to inspire." [13] Still another expresses "high hopes that these hymns for now will enrich your life, your faith, and your worship; and, most of all, a deeply felt wish that the songs of prayer, praise, thanksgiving, confession and exhortation which this book contains will be pleasing to God." [14]

117

Many of these introductions mention the role which the singing of hymns should play in the life of man and of the church. "One can only sing in the church, when one is really connected with the dynamic principles of history." [15] "Not only each generation . . . but all men bring off new worlds each week and every day. The culture is no longer a 'finished product.' Our ancestors did not do all the necessary creation. The only live culture is one on the make . . . one which is *becoming*." [16]

Many introductions also specify the ways hymns should be performed in church and describe the music of the hymns as expressions of all the moods prevailing in our lives: "Join with us, through these songs, in the vitality and bitterness, the doubt and fear, the joy and love, the humor and hope, found in the emerging church as it celebrates and represents the 'good news.'" [17]

Folk hymns or folk hymn settings constitute commercial music in that they are sold across the counter. They are profitable items for American business. Publishing houses have discovered that folk hymns appeal to thousands of church-going Americans. Music publishers have learned that successful folk hymns have to deal with things that interest young high school and college students—with religious, social, moral, and cultural ideals to which youth aspire. Publishers helped to create a ritualized world of the highly recognized folk-hymn arranger/producer who is sometimes also the folk hymn "troubadour," performing hymn tunes to guitar accompaniment. Folk hymns are established, institutionalized, official types of music of the church. Like the hymn tunes and settings of preceding centuries they occupy a definite place in the life of the church, i.e. to relate man to God and to edify him while doing so. With the sanction of the church young church people, through their folk hymns, are allowed to enter into the otherwise forbidden world of jazz, pop, and rock music.

The Black Contribution to the Folk Hymn

The "unification of perspectives" is culminated in the folk hymn by the addition of the musical characteristics of the black culture. The sounds and the texts of black spirituals are frequently used in the folk hymn books. The humming and moaning and groaning, a common mark of black music, becomes part of the singing style of the new folk hymn. This turns out to be a blissful or ecstatic rendition of a song, characterized by the full and free exploitation of melodic variation, sometimes with closed lips to create a humming effect.

The call-response principle of the black music appears in many refrain hymns. The relationship between a speaker, narrator, or singer, and the group, so common to black music, produces a strong sense of community participation.

Handclapping, common to blacks, appears in many folk hymns and provides percussive effects and maintains a rhythmic pulse for singing. Often clapping sounds constitute a regular offbeat. Variations of these schemes may result in syncopated rhythms.

In religious black music, singing and preaching often merged into one integral form. This style appears in *For Mature Adults Only* by Norman Habel and Richard Koehnecke, both white.

The religious songs of the blacks were often used as social comment. So are many new folk hymns by whites.

Black music plays a prime role in the establishment of the overall sound of the folk hymn. Its syncopations and feeling for a steady pulse beat are the crux of the new folk hymn. With the addition of the sound of the guitar, the folk hymn is a product of black and white America.

Together with the strong rhythmic and vital input of Afro-American music the new folk hymn participates in America's gift of its popular music to world music. This American popular music has grown out of the mixtures of European and African musical traditions. It is not buried in remote historical times like so much of European music, but is of recent vintage —like many things in America. This popular music is on the verge of becoming a western music of the 20th and perhaps of the 21st century.

As a part of this popular music, the folk hymn takes its historical place in continuation of the Roman hymn and sequence, the Lutheran chorale, and the gospel song of the white and black fundamentalist churches. The new hymn music overcomes the stagnation, decay, and decline in the creative production of significant, new, classical hymns. The change in hymn-making is similar to the changes in the political sphere, the destruction of the "old order" in World War I and the rise of the Third World out of World War II. The importance of black music for the rise of the new folk hymn should not be overlooked. Black music has contributed strongly to American popular music and to the new folk hymn as well.

9

Criteria for Evaluating New Church Music

We have described the new music, and we have learned that much of it is related to black music. Now we must ask ourselves, "How do we evaluate this new music?"

Basic to any evaluation is the affirmation that music is a language given to humans by the Creator. This is true for blacks and whites. There is no exclusive style of church music. Music derived from black culture, like the old classical music, comes into existence by the ongoing creative activity of God. An exclusive conception limits the materials available to the church musician and often opens the door for biased church leaders to pontificate, "De gustibus non disputandum est." This is an excuse to abandon their responsibility to develop an interest in new black-derived church music.

The psalmist encourages us to "Sing unto the Lord a new song." Black-derived church music is a new song. The new music expresses a special quality of celebration and unrestrained joy, yet these are not unique to the new church music. Even the apparently "new" dionysian element of *ekstasis* in black-derived church music is but another manifestation of the ecstatic quality of the soul music of the Moravians, the Amish, and the Hassidim.

The Texts: Some Theological Criteria

If we cannot evaluate the new church music by its adherence to one acceptable style, we must look to the message of the texts and to the musical quality of the new church music.

An example of theological content is Ray Repp's "The Easter Song." [1] It includes a combination of several theological aspects. "This is the day the Lord has made" expresses the adoration of God as the Creator of all of life. "Christians, sing to Christ our King, who's risen as he said" proclaims the message of grace as stated in the Good News of Jesus, who "conquered death today." "From now on we'll live anew" expresses hope in the promise of God for the future. The refrain and all five stanzas overflow with joy and thanksgiving for the blessings of God in Jesus Christ, "who's risen as he said." Love for all people and for all of creation is stated most prominently in "Trumpets, sound his message clear to earth and ev'ry land," Repp's 20th century Easter carol. The refrain and all five stanzas provide a system of theological relations in which attention is focused on the totality of Christ's love for us and our response of love for Christ and other people.

Not all texts of the new music are as obviously successful in expressing the Christian faith in the language of worship. However, when given the proper context and ideas for interpretation, hardly any of the new texts fail to provide at least one basic theological thought. For example, "Song for Psychedelia" by Lawrence Mohr[2] is introduced by the editor with these remarks:

> Here is a very heavy rock song about openness in relationships between people—the kind of openness which Christ makes possible for his body, the church.
> Through him all things were created, and in him all things are united; the barriers are falling, and we are free to move out beyond ourselves to love others.

Here is the text in its entirety:

> The barriers are falling
> And I hear the colors calling
> To go out, above, beyond myself,
> To see you, sense you, touch you where you are.
>
> The walls begin to crumble,
> And I hear your heartbreak rumble
> To come and find and share and merge,
> To sense, to see, to rise and leave the place you are
>
> Don't let the walls get in your way.
> Come on, bust 'em, smash 'em, break 'em,
> And hey, baby, don't remake them.
> We are living now in openness.
> The great light of each other fills our day.

The editors of *Hymns for Now,* I-III, believe that "the meaning a Christian brings to a song makes it 'sacred.' A song becomes a hymn when we interpret and use the words and melody to glorify God."

Judged on the basis of both text and context, I suggest at least four questions in examining the text of any

123

music, whether new music derived from the black culture, or new music composed in the classical church style, or old classical music.

Does the text express adoration to God as Lord of the church and all the world?

Many of the new hymns are most insistent on praising God in a contemporary world. In Sister Miriam Theresa Winter's "Changin'" God remains the same.[3] God is stability. God is the universal order amidst a changing environment, amidst man's changing ways of making a living, his changing dreams and ambitions. In "That's for me" God constitutes a repose to which men come and with which men have a "very happy day."[4] Many new hymns show God in a world which is obsessed by mobility. Gerald Beaumont's "There's a lot of good things in the earth" shows God in a Holiday Inn which is set up for all men and to which they may travel by air or by sea.[5] In Norman Habel's spacecraft hymn, "Christ is changing everything," the love for Christ's omnipresence and power is coordinated with the exultation of man—God's creature—and man's own endeavors in space: "I know we spin on earth beneath a dancing sky. . . . I sense an unseen world beyond the swirling sun."[6] "It's a long road to freedom" is a characteristic example of a backpack-hiking hymn of adoration: "I walked one morning by the sea."[7] So is the Medical Mission Sisters' "Pilgrim Song."[8]

Some new adoration hymns see man, who is maker and producer of the technological society in which he lives, as a child of God. Man likes to return to a childlike simplicity in his relationship with God, relying on God alone in a world of hatred and imprisonment, as expressed in "Take my hand."[9] "There's changes at the door" reveals man's dependence on God in a world which is changing.[10] "Keep me true" exposes that same dependence in a world which is false and corrupt.[11] Man's longing for sweet, paternal love, refreshment, and repose is illustrated touchingly in "How I have longed." [12]

Does the text rejoice in the presence of Christ in the present time of human culture as well as in past ages?

Some Christians like to identify themselves with the entire history of Christianity. They like to use the old to interpret the new. This desire is reflected in many of the new hymns. Sister Germaine borrows the refrain, "From among the branches," from Psalm 104:-12.[13] Stephen Leddy's "Everybody's cryin' out" reminds us of Psalm 130, "Out of the depths I cry to thee." [14]

Historical consciousness is not longing after past times. Rather, history is consciousness of an ongoing and living tradition that is not dead or petrified, but which is going on, even at the present moment. For Sister Germaine and Stephen Leddy the psalm text is very much alive. It helps to vitalize, illuminate, and interpret the present. Acknowledgement of the presence of Christ through time creates a new consciousness of history that includes past, present, and future events as well. James Ooting's "The happening" is a proud song of "The sounds of a new generation" which "will echo throughout history." [15]

Don Wyrtzen cries for a soapbox, from which he wants to proclaim the story of the death and resurrection of Christ. "O give me a soapbox" revitalizes the image of "O give me a home" of a past century.[16] Many new hymns express the hope of renewal and social justice. Sonny Salsbury's "Jesus was just a good guy" portrays the Christ of 2000 years ago and the Christ of today:

Jesus was another revolutionary . . .
He said some things that the brass did not like . . .
But why did he die on a tree
And say that he did it for me? [17]

Social justice is the motto in the anti-racist song, "Who's that guy":

Who's that guy . . .
Who's that guy with the beard? . . .
He's awful dark.
Is he Black or White? . . .
He looks Jewish . . .
Hey, look at his hands!
Why, they're bleeding! [18]

God is a personal God in John E. Walvoord's "We fought a jungle war today." [19] The violence of the war and the shadows of the night are overcome by Christ, "who joined the jungle war one day/nailed on a cross to pay man's way." Our world of social, political, racial, and economic problems will be helped by the ever-present love of Christ, who "once had a plan that showed us how to live together." "This plan was the place of love, more than we've got." So writes Kurt Kaiser in his hymn, "It's our world." [20]

Many of the new hymns like to show Christ's presence in actual life today. They are the expression of an unsophisticated, uncritical, and inarticulate people, very often through the use of idiomatic and vernacular language. Expressions such as, "It's a groove," "Gee, you're right," "Hey! What's the matter with you," are frequent. Some of these new hymns have helped non-middle-class Americans express themselves spiritually.

Does the text express thanksgiving for the blessings of God?

Sister Germaine's "From among the branches" is an exemplary "Bless the Lord" kind of hymn.[21] Man is not only grateful for the mountains and rivers God has given him, but also for the records and telephones, picnics and parties, basketballs and volleyballs, and all the paraphernalia of American family life.

People are thankful for specific blessings of God, such as the sense of hearing, seeing, and touching. Without these blessings it would be impossible to say thanks to God. We should want to use these senses in a keener way to become more aware of the power of listening and of singing: "Heaven's gates will open wide; I've got a reason to sing." [22] If we did not have the senses given by God—the senses of hearing and seeing—how could we ever tell the story that "Christ is changing everything": [23]

> I *hear* a word from God that frees a man to fly . . .
> I *hear* the tulips laugh beneath the winter snow . . .
> I've *seen* how little children make their parents grow . . .
> I *sense* an *unseen* world beyond the swirling sun
> I *look* for mysteries that haven't yet begun.

The story of the entire hymn, "What people," is based on the accuracy of a visual experience: "When you've *looked* in the street lately, did you really *see* people there?" [24] Without a visual experience the Christian would not be aware of the "darkness of the world" or of "bright an' shining faces," of which we read in M. R. McGervey's "Have you got soul?" [25] The sense of touch is represented in Charles F. Brown's "Reach out and touch." [26] Many hymns contain this element of touching, of reaching out for souls that are hungry, of communicating through Christ. Communication to form a *Gemeinschaft* in place of our *Gesellschaft* is the main theme in Peter Scholte's "They'll know we are Christians by our love." [27] "We will work with each other, we will work side by side" doxologizes communal spirit above everything. Communication has to be established with everybody. The "I" of Toplady's "Rock of ages" and the "we" of Luther's "A mighty fortress" have been changed to "Everybody's cryin' out" in Stephen Leddy's "This is what you're looking for." [28]

Does the text express supplication and love for all people and for all creation of God?

New love hymns are in abundance. Love for all people is approached by many routes. They all lead to belief that love should not be restricted to the Sunday service within the walls of the church. Sometimes the new love hymns may encompass God's love for the representatives of the animal kingdom, no matter how small. "The woolly lamb jumpin' in a field" and "a sparrow lyin' dead on a field" are included.[29] In David Collyer's "What people" [30] the frame of reference of love is expanded to factory workers, to men in the city and in suburbia, in Africa and in India. A love hymn, such as "In a silent world," goes beyond the steeples of the church to the transmitter towers of the mass media. Through the mass media we may find the love we are searching for: "Then a seeking world through the Savior's care will have love to share with men ev'rywhere in a humble world." [31] Most frequently the point of the story of the new love hymn is the fact that Christians are known by their urgent communality of sharing love for each other and for men in need, such as expressed in "They'll know we are Christians" [32] and "Reach out and touch";[33] that this love should shine for all people, as proclaimed in "Shine";[34] and that this love should help us to overcome racial prejudices, wars, loneliness and hatred, as revealed in Kent Schneider's *Songs for Celebration*.

The Music: Some Criteria

We have previously stated that a new black-derived hymn is acceptable to us only when it provides a text which is theologically sound, that is, capable of reinforcing and recasting certain basic theological truths. Sound theology alone, however, will not move the mind and heart unless it is accompanied by a good melody.

In the classical chorales or the new church hymns, a good melody occurs whenever certain rationales of melodic hymn tune constructon are observed.

Good melodic construction is provided when balance between melodic tone steps is present.

Typically, small intervals between tones characterize hymn tunes. Tunes of this character are utilitarian in that they can be easily sung by any member of the congregation. Thus, simple hymn melodies tend to support the message of the text. When larger intervallic skips occur in a melody, they will usually be balanced by smaller tone steps either preceding or following them at a "proper" time interval. A pattern of stepwise tones serves to mollify the potent expressive quality of a melodic leap of a sixth or octave. "All the world's a seeker," by Karen Moshier, combines convincingly a pearl-string melody of ascending step progressions and the gentle roll of larger ascending and descending intervals:[35]

All the world's a __ seek - er   won-d'ring where   to   go.

Some melodies are the product of their accompanying harmony. Such melodies are simply near representations of various chord progressions, and are thus, in a sense, "harmonic melodies." Many folk hymns, for example, chime out the intervals of the basic triad.

129

Ray Repp's "All you people, clap your hands" is a beautiful illustration.[36]

Other melodies are determined or expanded by the particular mode in which they are cast. A "gapped" scale, such as the one used in the ballad, "The Lord brooded over land and sea," causes a balanced exchange of skip and step progressions: [37]

Good melodic construction is provided when rhythmical balance is present.

Rhythm serves to further the melodic balance of the hymn in the new church. As in black music, syncopation and shifting rhythmic accents in the black-derived hymn posit the principles of order and structure within a tune. Don Wyrtzen's rhythmic structure of the first measures of "O give me a soapbox" points to this aspect rather clearly: [38]

O give me a soap-box and___ I'll stand up and say,___

The three rhythmic shifts on the notes B-flat, G, and E-flat lend a certain swing and impetus to the melody without turning it upside down. The rhythmic prolongation of the last note gives repose and rest, establishing fully the primacy of the whole note beat over all other beats.

Good melodic construction is provided when motivic balance is present.

The new hymn tunes are usually made up of only a few motives. Robert Blue's "Run, come see" is comprised of only one motive.[39]

All: Run, come, see Ch: the seed a crack-in'. All: Run, come, see Ch: it crack-in' now.

In some tunes one particular motive will give a specific thrust to the entire tune. In Ralph Carmichael's "I heard about," for example, the initial motive is a potent generator for the tune to follow: [40]

I heard a-bout old No-ah, land-in' on the

moun-tain top I heard a-bout old 'Zek-iel

preach-in' to the bones; but great-er than all these

mir-a-cles is some-thing that hap-pened to me that day that

Je-sus came in-to my heart to stay. ___

131

Good melodic construction is provided when formal balance is present.

As in the established hymn tune, musical form is of key significance for the new hymn. Among the formal schemes of the new hymns is the bar form, which in Carmichael's "I heard about" is used very convincingly. Still other traditional forms of the established hymn repertory prevail in the new hymns. In addition, the many new hymn refrain structures have made a distinct and significant contribution as is evidenced by many of Ray Repp's tunes.

A good and a bad hymn tune

Before we sit in judgment on the suitability of a hymn tune, we must be aware that the beauty of the tune is based on the sum of all its musical elements: melody, rhythm, motivic work, and form. A good hymn tune, therefore, is a good job of musical engineering. Whenever one element is deficient, the entire tune suffers. In such an instance, the clockwork of melodic energy, rhythmic drive, motivic interaction, and formal synthesis does not work properly.

As an example of musical elements working together, consider "First Place." [41] Many protagonists of exclusively traditional church music would find this hymn unacceptable because of its unassuming, schmaltzy, poplike melody, its waltz beat, and its lack of virility and robustness. Actually, this tune is a gem of new black-derived folk hymns. It meets all the musical criteria a tune should meet. The repeated tones in the opening phrase of the hymn are balanced effectively by relatively large intervallic skips toward the end of the tune. The waltz rhythm is modified by the basic pattern, which is a variation of the waltz pattern *per se.* Motivic changes yield melodic variety and keep

132

the tune rolling within the frame of a two-part song form.

Examine, on the other hand, the following hymn, "He's listening," by Flo Price: [42]

No one knows what a smile can con - ceal, but

God un - der - stands what a young heart feels

This tune carries the virtue of simple stepwise melodic progressions too far. The melody opens with a repeated note pattern, which is relieved by only limited stepwise progressions. It lacks any significant contrasts to interrupt the monotony established in the opening phrase. The harmonization of the guitar-inspired accompaniment supplies the only relief, but even this is unable to erase the basic weakness of the tune. Nor is the monotony helped by the persistent pattern of the slow waltz rhythm. To be sure, waltz rhythms are not inherently dull. Consider the initial motive in Johann Strauss' "Emperor Waltz":

The vigorous rhythmic pattern of this piece is alive with subtle rhythmic changes, four changes occurring within the first four measures! The two motives which comprise the entire Price hymn are very weak. Thus, they contribute little to the quality of the tune. Furthermore, the motivic elaboration is based on repetition exclusively. There is very little evidence of musical invention or logic. Since the weak qualities outweigh the strong ones, this tune, unlike the Spurr example, does not fulfill the criteria of hymn tune rationality.

133

Postlude

In conclusion, we can make some generalizations about evaluating the new church song. Broadly speaking, we have applied fundamental criteria to the significance of the text and to the intrinsic quality of the music. Texts have been judged to be appropriate if they fulfill certain theological qualifications which are expansively conceived and liberally applied. They may explore the meaning of Christ's message as it has evolved to the understanding of modern man, and of the Christian life as it has reached into every phase of modern man's existence. Thus, the new church song communicates the significance of Christian life in the 20th century of the fullest possible extent. The matter of judging the appropriateness of the texts demands an enlightened and expansive understanding of Christianity as a moving and living force in the modern world. We have noted that some of the new hymns are not explicit in their setting forth of the Christian faith, that is, they make no *direct* reference to God, to Christ, or to the church. Such songs therefore depend on their context for their theological significance. However, when provided the setting of a worship service and a Christian interpretation they generally serve admirably in illuminating and vitalizing classic Christian concepts.

The task of evaluating the music is more problematical. A specialized skill is involved. We have tried to explore some standards of musical quality by which to judge the repertory of the new black-derived church song. These standards represent only an initial approach to the problem of what is good in church music. Given the difficulty of making value judgments regarding music, it is not surprising to see the church seeking a haven in the realms of antique music that

134

bears the imprimatur of approval from past generations. While it hardly seems reasonable for the church to limit itself to antique liturgies or baroque-style cathedrals, yet this unreasonable approach is often suggested and vigorously defended by church leaders in regard to music.

If we accept the principle that the music of today has a place in the church, then we must use some evaluative criteria. Even at this acceptance, however, we must realize that no criteria can bear the entire burden for the task of evaluating music. Ultimately, the value and significance of music transcends all rational criteria. The ways in which music carries spiritual meaning are ultimately religious and mystical. An extraordinary work, such as Beethoven's Ninth Symphony, illustrates this capacity. While Beethoven's work fulfills many of the criteria of well-made music, its power transcends these criteria. The real value of this music is its capacity to communicate intangible values. This capacity is evident, however, only in the effect which the music has on the listener. At the other end of the spectrum are many works, which, while they fulfill all the criteria for well-made music, are ultimately insignificant. Their insignificance is evident in their deficiency to communicate anything more than a musical skeleton.

Thus, measureable criteria provide only one way to evaluate music and therefore can provide only a first step for evaluating the new black-derived church music. Beyond the strictly musical grammatical elements, a hymn's evaluation becomes a personal matter, a subjective judgment about the capacity of the hymn to communicate meaning. For this step, there are no final canons of measurement. Our American composer, Charles Ives, had this ultimate personal evaluation of music in mind when he described the value of gospel hymns for the common man:

These hymns have for him (the man born down to Babbit's Corners) a truer ring than many of those groove-made, even-measured, monotonous, non-rhythmed, indoor-smelling, priest-taught, academic, English or neo-English hymns (and anthems)—well written, well harmonized things, well-voice-led, well counterpointed, well corrected, and well O.K.'d by well corrected Mus. Bac. F.O.G.'s—personified sounds, correct and inevitable to sight and hearing; in a word, those proper forms of stained-glass beauty which our over-drilled mechanisms-boys choirs—are limited to.

10

The Future of
Church Music in America

The future of American church music depends to a large degree on the willingness of Americans to consider the necessity for change. This willingness may become somewhat easier when Americans try to understand that a piece of church music which is now considered classic, static, and established was once new and revolutionary. Indeed, it could never have come into existence if some support for its innovating source had not been available. This support for the new and dynamic should become obvious to Americans when they see American church music as a product of American culture, rather than a continuation of European culture—however important the latter has been.

This willingness to accept change implies also a willingness to create new material, even if much of this material is a "rehash'" of something that previously existed. Many things connected with the black-derived hymn have had a prior existence in American church music. Moreover, they have previously proved themselves acceptable to large segments of the church population in this country. For these reasons, there is little rationale (and indeed, one would have to be a racist) for opposing a 1970 version of something that not only existed in 1870 American culture, but was then appreciated by American parishioners.

Church Music—A Lot of "Trash"

Many of the melodies of black-derived hymns are musical "trash" when seen from the ramparts of the classical church music of Palestrina, Bach, Bruckner, and Penderecki. While the melodies of these great masters move within elaborations of relatively large-scale works, the melodies of the black-derived hymns make up short, self-contained entities. While the melodies of the above-mentioned composers are aimed toward a relatively sophisticated audience, the black-derived hymn is directed toward the rhythmically-obedient "in-the-pew" listener, who hears the beat, the "underlying, unabating time unit of the music," which mimics the unabating machine-rhythms ruling his life.[1] Classicism, on the other hand, is attained through other means: through linear extension and rhythmic balance in the motets and masses of Palestrina, through effective individualization in the works of Bach, Bruckner, and Penderecki.

Church Music—Homo Ludens

Americans have a conservative attitude toward their church music. They avoid changes and innovations and like to attach themselves to traditional sound-making. Traditional sound production is indebted to folk and popular music practices, for example, the deliberate cutting, arranging, and adjusting of classical church music masterpieces, such as Handel's *Messiah* or Dubois' *Seven Last Words;* also, the transposing of compositions, when necessary, to any suitable pitch. Congregations sing their hymns to dotted rhythms and syncopated beats. March-like meters are preferred.

All of these elements of folk and popular music practices in church music are just another facet of man's belief that all of life, including church art and music, is a kind of "game" or "play," that includes the possibility of great seriousness *(serio ludere).* According to Huizinga, this type of "play" operates according to four criteria: 1) that the "play" is free, that it is, in fact, freedom; 2) that the "play" is not "ordinary" or "real" life, but that it is a kind of illusion; 3) that the "play" is distinct from "ordinary" life with regard to locality and duration and is "played out" within certain limits of time and place; 4) and that the "play" creates order, in fact, that it *is* order, and that "that order is dependent on strictly observed rules and sanctions." [2]

These elements of play are observed in the traditional liturgies of the western churches. They are also capsuled in the gospel song of the 19th century, in the church music of the blacks, and in the black-derived hymn of our present society. The element of "playing out" is at hand: 1) in improvization; 2) in the "playing out" of a written note when a piece is recorded rather than adhering to its literal form; 3) in the use of rhythms borrowed from popular and black-derived music; and 4) in the juxtaposition of various styles and art forms, as, for example, in Bernstein's Mass. Order in the music of this mass is present: 1) when each instrument is given equal time for an improvization of a service that employs jazz instrumentalists; 2) when the guitar replaces the organ, creating a more democratic (vs. authoritarian) relationship between the accompanying instrument and the congregation, choir, or solo singer; 3) when the black call-and-response pattern is used; and 4) when rock music and traditional music are combined.

Church Music—Ecstatic Quality

Many of the black-derived hymns, like many of the old gospel songs, take the singer out of his ordinary day-to-day existence to what might be conceived of as "a different world." The singing of the black-derived hymn, like the singing of the gospel songs, leads to a change of consciousness characterized by intense excitement. Members of congregations need the kind of spiritual excitement the gospel song and the black-derived hymn provide. After having their consciousness altered, their spirits relieved, and their souls temporarily and religiously lifted up, people are better prepared to return to the mundane "everydayness" of reality.

Church Music's Melodic Quality

The impression one gains of black-derived folk, pop, jazz, rock, and church music is that it moves on the same tracks as traditional church music, that it is actually not so new and different, that it has been "said before." Ray Repp's "Allelu," for example, is on the same wave length as Bradbury's "Just as I am" or Lowry's "Shall we gather at the river." The black-derived hymn is like some of the gospel songs, in which Charles Ives found

> a vigor, a depth of feeling, a natural soul rhythm, a sincerity—which in spite of a vociferous sentimentality, carries him nearer the "Christ of the

people" than does the Te Deum of the greatest cathedral.[3]

Black-derived Hymns—A Part of the Spiritual Song Repertoire

Since the black-derived hymn moves along in the mainstream of America's hymn culture, it is forming a part of the already existing spiritual song repertoire. The spiritual song consists of the Sunday school hymn, the black and white spiritual, the black and white gospel song, black soul music, the vast body of sacred solo music, and blues and rock songs that contain religious themes.

The marvelous productivity, ingenuity, and drive of the American people has produced an abundance of black-derived hymn material. These black derivations are being tried, examined, rejected, accepted, and absorbed by a large body of American church denominations and movements. They have amplified and enriched the already existing repertory of the spiritual song and will continue to do so.

Five Church-Music Cultures

The black-derived hymn is only a part of a larger unit that includes a variety of different musico-cultural traditions. In addition to traditional-contemporary church-music cultures there are five distinct music cultures: 1) the standard hymnbook culture; 2) the spiritual song culture; 3) the spontaneous spiritual song culture; 4) the historistic church music culture; and 5) the multi-media church music culture. All of these cultures exist simultaneously. All contain elements that demand their continuance.

The standard hymnbook culture stands for the maintenance, promotion, and defense of tradition, liturgical place, and order.

The spiritual song culture may seem to stand for the opposite, the a-traditional, non-orderly, and irrational. However, as said before, it is in line with the gospel song tradition which has a venerable place in the "hall of fame" of church music in America. It contains the fresh and invigorating rhythms and sounds of God's world outside the church.

The spontaneous spiritual song culture is closely related to the roots of black gospel music in that it allows communal participation and creation.

The historistic church music culture stresses the beauty and meaningfulness of liturgical music of the Renaissance and Baroque eras, that is, European and non-black music. These compositions have become available through the research of musicologists and ethno-musicologists in the last fifty years.

The multi-media church music culture is a result of our advancement in technological productions. It draws its musical material from the preceding four cultures. It is still in an exploratory period but it has great possibilities.

The Future of American Church Music

Forecast 1: The spiritual song culture will continue to expand.

I foresee that the spiritual song culture will continue to expand. Americans are in the process of reviving the great black music of the past. We are witnessing at the moment a phenomenal renaissance of ragtime music. We will see a flood of performances of the late Duke Ellington's works. His extraordinary achievements for music in America and in the world will be increasingly recognized. His various sacred compositions, already quite popular, will become still more so. The increasing use of great serious music by black popular composers will have an impact on the production of black-derived hymn materials.

I do not foresee, however, that Americans will become more aware of the intrinsic artistic qualities of the compositions of these black musicians, or more sensitive to the impact of blackness on American music. They will continue to listen to black music, to black-derived hymns, without acknowledging the corresponding ethnic roots and significance. They will continue to insulate themselves against the outside-world realities of the spiritual song repertoire and be shut up in the ghetto walls built by academically acceptable hymns.

Forecast 2: Racism in church music will not easily disappear.

Racism is a key issue in the discussion of church music of the past, present, and future in America. I foresee that it will not easily disappear. It has held a strong foothold for many centuries in American church music.

According to John Wesley, Isaac Watts' *Hymns and Spiritual Songs* (1709) had great appeal for the southern blacks. However, an analysis of the texts of many of Watts' hymns reveals a racist perspective. No matter how noble the intentions of the author, many of Watts' texts served as devices for racial control and for maintaining the status quo of slavery. *The Hymns and Spiritual Songs* conveyed a major concept of conduct that undoubtedly made a deep impression on the slave. Many of Watts' texts offered the vicarious experience of satisfaction through servile, meek, and submissive conduct—conduct which, to a once proud people, must have seemed both humiliating and degrading.

143

Blest is the man whose shoulders take
My yoke, and bear it with delight;
My yoke is easy to his neck,
My grace shall make the burden light.

A discussion on church and racism must also include the problem of anti-semitism and church music. Friedrich Blume's article on "Musik und Rasse," for example, provides significant insights into the cast of racial arguments and the employment of Darwinian metaphors in the musico-cultural realm. In his attempt to establish a distinctly Nordic-Germanic music, Blume, the author of the most authoritative work on the history of Lutheran music in Germany, asserts that J. S. Bach's *Art of the Fugue* allows for the intuition of the energy and heroic greatness of the "Nordic" soul and that this particular intuition is caused by the austerity and strictness of form in the work. To counteract any notion that might tie the German Baroque to developments in Italy or France, to deny any possible dependency on musical developments outside the space of the Nordic race, Blume proceeds to invoke the argument of the dominant strength and character of the Nordic people. No comment about anti-semitism and church music is necessary when one of the foremost German musicologists, the editor of the monumental music encyclopedia, *Die Musik in Geschichte und Gegenwart,* proclaims the superiority of one race over another.

Forecast 3: The movement to promote and cultivate church music of the past will expand.

Church music historicism is an ongoing movement. Together with the expansion of church musicology, church music historicism is sure to expand. Church music historicism was made possible through the phenomenal rise of musicology in the United States since the end of World War II. Many "renaissances" of composers of the past, for example Schütz, Handel, Telemann, have occurred. An increasing number of collegia-musica groups perform the music of these great masters in church and college auditoriums. Church musicians have become increasingly aware of the great variety, flexibility, and creativity involved in the performances of this music. Many harpsichordists, lutenists, and guitarists perform Renaissance and Baroque music on new, often American-built, instruments. The number of recorder players of all ages and performance abilities is increasing.

The invasion of Renaissance and Baroque music has created a musical class that considers this music superior to any other. For example, the music of Johann Walther, Ludwig, Senfl, and Balthasar Resinarius, in addition to the above-mentioned composers, is considered superior to the music of an F. Melius Christiansen.

This same musical class lends its ear also to the sound of 20th century German and German-American composers, such as Ernst Pepping, Hugo Distler, Jan Bender, and Ludwig Lenel, whose compositional techniques are essentially indebted to the modern application of contrapuntal and concertizing crafts found in the Renaissance and Baroque masterworks. This same musical class will also favor the church music of such American composers as Daniel Moe, whose works must also be understood in the light of the historistic movement.

Forecast 4: Historicism will also affect American church music development.

Musicological studies in the United States have finally touched also on the study of American music and American church music.

A great example of the application of historistic principles to composition was given by the great pioneer figure of modern American music, Henry Cowell (1897-1965). Like the great Brazilian composer, Heitor Villa-Lobos (1887-1959), who combined in his *Bachianas Brasileiras* Brazilian rhythms and sounds with the Baroque techniques of J. S. Bach, Henry Cowell in his *Hymns and Fuguing Tunes* replaced the prelude-fugue constellation of Bach by a different bisectional organization, using the hymn for the prelude and the Anglo-American fuguing tune for the fugue. Some of Cowell's hymns and fuguing tunes are symphonies (Nos. 4, 6, 7, 9, and 10), others are pieces for band (No. 1), string orchestra (Nos. 2 and 5), and chamber orchestra (No. 16).

The establishment of the Society for Ethnomusicology opened the doors to investigations of "folk," "primitive," and "pop" music and instruments of many countries and lands. Perhaps an impact of ethnomusicological studies is the rare inclusion of a *Gaguku* (Japanese) melody in the Presbyterian hymnal, *Worship Book*. Although the church has little place for nonwestern melodies in its hymnals, American school children are exposed to non-western music through the many examples of music school texts, such as the *New Dimension in Music* series, published by the American Book Company, 1970.

Forecast 5: Black-derived music will have a catalytic effect on historicism.

I foresee that black-derived church music will "jell" with the historistic interest in Renaissance and Baroque music and in music of the American past. Contrapuntal writing, linear projection, is one of the key techniques applied in some of Nadia Boulanger's American students, such as Aaron Copland and Roy Harris. Elliott

146

Carter has given us in his funny choral piece, "Musicians wrestle everywhere," a showpiece of Renaissance madrigal technique. At the same time, both Copland and Harris have been able to merge the popular or pragmatic with the classical or contrapuntal in their war-years compositions, "Lincoln Portrait" and "The Folk Symphony," respectively. This merging will happen, since the performance of Renaissance and Baroque music has brought forth a stress on the concertizing style, that is, a style which stresses the playful element in music. This element of *ludere* is also present in American church music practices in general and in black-derived church music practices in particular.

The Chicago University Divinity School theologian, Joseph Sittler, taking a part in a Faith and Life Institute on Jazz and Contemporary Culture, once made the point that "play," having fun, is one of the most revelatory activities of a human being. The concept of play is not a frivolous one; it is the center. Rite, ritual, dance, folk-expression in play form, all common action in joyous rhythmic participation, that is, liturgy, is at the heart of man's existence.[4]

Music culture of the young in America has often been exposed to a variety of musical insinuations. Rock music has taken ideas from modern classical music, from folk and pop music, from the black "blues." One particular composer of classical music was able to celebrate the fresh original vision only young people, and only a few young people, possess. Henry Cowell remained as open as any young man to every musical possibility. He started with what he heard while young, the marvelous eclecticism of his California surroundings combining the Irish songs and dances of his father, the Iowa folk songs of his mother, the sounds of the sea, and the Chinese opera. He incorporated whatever had been done anywhere in the world, from the 18th century Billings' hymns and fuguing tunes to Iranian music. I foresee that America's youth will increasingly step into Cowell's footsteps, using materials from the nonwestern world as well as black sources for their spiritual songs.

Leonard Bernstein, the perennial friend of music of the young and of American popular music, understood this when he composed his Mass, a genuine musical garden in which all sorts of black-derived music were mixed with music of the Reformation, Baroque, and modern eras.

I foresee that youth will increasingly participate in the shaping of the spiritual song repertoire. This activity will eventually cross the ways of historistic church music. Both activities will occur to the accompaniment of the black-derived hymn and service music.

I foresee that we will fulfill the words which the great Franz Liszt wrote once in relationship to the needs of expansion of church music in his own time:

> Nowdays when the altar is trembling and tottering, when pulpit and religious ceremony serve as subject matter for the mockers and skeptics, art must forsake the holy of holies, expand itself, and seek a stage for its magnificent manifestation in the world outside.
>
> How often—indeed, how much more than often —music must acknowledge both people and God as its springs of life. It needs to hasten from one to the other, in order to ennoble, comfort, and chasten mankind as well as to bless and praise God.[5]

NOTES

Chapter 1

1. Tony Heilbut, *The Gospel Sound* (New York, 1971), p. 10.
2. Alan Lomax, "The Homogeniety of Afro-American Musical Style," *Afro-American Anthropology*, ed. by Norman E. Whitten, Jr. and John F. Szwed (New York, 1970), p. 197. For additional information read Lovell, John Jr., *Black Song: The Forge and the Flame* (New York, 1972).
3. James M. Trotter, *Music and Some Highly Musical People* (1891).
4. Cp. words at the end of the first scene "your heart, your heart."

Chapter 2

1. It would be perhaps more appropriate to describe this sense of regular pulse in African music in terms of the human pulse rather than in terms of a device of modern technological society.
2. *Service Book and Hymnal* (1958), 262.
3. Hans Joachim Moser, *Heinrich Schütz*, translated and edited by Derek Mulloch (London, 1967), p. 56.

4. Rose Brandel, *The Music of Central Africa* (The Hague, 1961), p. 49.
5. Rose Brandel, p. 67.
6. Rose Brandel, p. 67.
7. Rose Brandel, p. 67.
8. Cp. recording of *Music of the Princes of Dahomey—Festival of the Tohossou,* Counterpoint 537.

Chapter 3

1. Improvisation was only tolerated in the American Calvinist/Puritan churches. The comprehension of the message of the spiritual text was of greater significance to them than the pleasurability of the act of singing. By contrast, the Afro-American churches enthusiastically cultivated musical improvisation.
2. LeRoi Jones, *Blues People* (New York, 1963), pp. 44-45.
3. Fredrick Law Olmsted, "A Journal to the Seaboard Slave States," (1856) quoted in Harvey Wish, ed., *Slavery in the South* (New York, 1964), pp. 201-202.
4. Charlotte Forten, "Life on the Sea Islands," quoted in Harvey Wish, ed., *Slavery in the South* (New York, 1964), pp. 95-96.
5. Arthur Ramos, *O Folclore Negro do Brasil* (Rio de Janeiro, 1954), p. 139.
6. José Teixeira d' Assumpcao, *Curso de Folclore Musical Brasileiro* (Rio de Janeiro, 1967), p. 82.
7. The term *candomblé* has various meanings: 1) All of Afro-American religions; 2) the location where a candomblé takes place; 3) Let us have a candomblé!

Chapter 4

1. LeRoi Jones, *Blues People* (New York, 1963), p. 219.
2. LeRoi Jones, p. 165.
3. W. E. B. DuBois, *The Souls of Black Folk* (Greenwich, Conn., 1961).
4. W. E. B. DuBois, Preface.
5. W. E. B. DuBois, Chapter 9.

6. W. E. B. DuBois, p. 181.
7. W. E. B. DuBois, p. 192.
8. J. F. Szwed, "Musical Adaptations among Afro-Americans," *Journal of American Folklore* (April-June 1969), pp. 112 ff.
9. Tony Heilbut, *The Gospel Sound: Good News and Bad Times* (New York, 1971), p. 282, 288.
10. Tony Heilbut, p. 288.
11. Heilbut, p. 121.
12. Heilbut, p. 322.
13. More on gospel song: William H. Tallmadge, "Dr. Watts and Mahalia Jackson," *Ethnomusicology*, V, No. 2 (May 1961), pp. 95-99.
14. "Run, Old Jeremiah," recorded at State Prison Farm, Jennings, Louisiana, 1934, Library of Congress (LC) 102, *Archive of American Folk Songs* (AAFS) 12B.

Chapter 5

1. John H. Mueller, "The Aesthetic Experience and Sociological Man," *Journal of Music Therapy* (March 1964), p. 12.
2. Quoted in Oskar Söhngen, "Theologische Grundlagen der Kirchenmusik" in *Leiturgia, Handbuch des Evangelischen Gottesdienstes,* Vol. IV *Die Musik des Evangelischen Gottesdienstes,* ed. by Karl Ferdinand Müller and Walter Blankenburg (Kassel, 1961), p. 92.
3. Quoted in Walter H. Kemp, *"Dietrich Bonhoeffer's 'Polyphony of Life,'"* Church Music (70/1), p. 15.
4. Christian Bunners, *Kirchenmusik und Seelenmusik, Studien zur Frömmigkeit und Musik im Luthertum des 17. Jahrhunderts* (Göttingen, 1966), p. 154.
5. Christian Bunners, p. 138.
6. Joseph Warren Yoder, *Amische Lieder* (Huntington, Pa., 1942), V.
7. Ibid.
8. Yoder, p. 40.
9. Yoder, V.
10. *Service Book and Hymnal* (Minneapolis, 1958), p. 7.

11. Julius Sachse, "The Diaries of Magister Johannes Kelpius," *Proceedings and Addresses, Pennsylvania German Society* (Lancaster, Pa., 1917), p. 60.

12. Julius Sachse, *Justus Falckner, Mystic and Scholar* (Philadelphia, Pa.), p. 46.

13. Ammon Monroe Aurand, *Historical Account of the Ephrata Cloister and the Seventh Day Baptist Society* (Harrisburg, 1940), p. 15.

14. Ibid, p. 23.

15. This is hymn 28, a dialogue of Brethren and Sisters in Edward D. Andrews, *The Gift to Be Simple: Songs, Dances and Rituals of the American Shakers* (New York, 1940), pp. 42, 43.

16. Juan B. Rael, *The New Mexican Alabad* (Palo Alto, 1951).

17. Rael, p. 22.

18. Rael, p. 139.

Chapter 6

1. John Rublowsky, *Popular Music* (New York, 1967), p. 150.

Chapter 7

1. See *Time,* Sept. 20, 1971, p. 42.

2. J. M. Leclerc, *Misa Tepozteca* (Cuernavaca, 1966), p. 9.

3. Leclerc, p. 11.

4. Leclerc, p. 172.

5. Leclerc, p. 173.

6. Leclerc, p. 172.

7. Francis W. Mahoney, "The Aymara Indians: A Model for Liturgical Adaptation," *Worship* 47, No. 2, pp. 405-413.

Chapter 8

1. *Risk, New Hymns for a New Day,* Vol. II, 3 (Geneva, Switzerland, 1966), pp. 21-23.

2. See Edward A. Sovik, *Architecture for Worship* (Minneapolis, 1973).

152

3. Grote Gottfried, ed. Heinrich Schütz, *Cantiones Sacrae,* 1625. Bärenreiter Edition. (Kassel, 1955) p. 90.

4. Wüllner, Franz, ed. Johann Sebastian Bach, *Werke,* Vol. 33 (17) Bach Gesellschaft (Leipzig, 1887), p. 117.

5. Carlton R. Young, *Song Book for Saints and Sinners* (Chicago, 1971) p. 26.

6. Ed Summerlin, *Contemporary Music for Congregations* (Madison, Wis.) p. 26.

7. Ewald Bash and John Ylvisaker, *Songs for Today* (Minneapolis, 1964), p. 35.

8. Young, p. 6.

9. Young, p. 4.

10. *Contemporary Worship I*—Hymns (Minneapolis, 1969), Preface.

11. Young, p. 4.

12. *Trial Music for Contemporary Worship,* Music Commission, Diocese of Mass., 1969.

13. Risk, *New Hymns for a New Day,* 1966.

14. Martin W. Steyer, *Hymns for Now III,* 1972.

15. Risk, *New Hymns for a New Day,* 1966, Preface.

16. Kent Schneider, *Songs for Celebration,* 1969.

17. Young, p. 4.

Chapter 9

1. *Come Alive with Ray Repp,* F. E. L. Publications, Chicago, 1967, p. 15.

2. Martin W. Steyer, Richard M. Koehnecke, ed., *Hymns for Now III,* Concordia Publishing House (St. Louis, 1972) No. 6.

3. Sister Miriam Theresa Winter, *Knock, Knock,* Vanguard (1968) p. 14.

4. Kurt Kaiser, "That's for Me" in *(More) Folk (Songs) for (Young) Folk,* Sacred Songs, (Waco, Texas, 1969) p. 3.

5. Fr. Gerard Beaumont, "There's a lot of good things in the earth" in *27 20th Century New Words, New Music* by members of the 20th Century Church Light Music Group, Josef Weinberger (London, 1965) p. 39.

6. Norman Habel, Resources for Youth Ministry, 10/69, Vol. I, No. 3, *Hymns for Now II,* 1969, No. 14.

7. The Medical Mission Sisters, *Joy Is Like the Rain,* Vanguard (1965) No. 6, p. 8.

8. The Medical Mission Sisters, *Joy Is Like the Rain,* Vanguard (1965) No. 8, p. 10.

9. Twila Hayes, "Take my hand" in Peter Scholtes, *They'll Know We Are Christians by Our Love,* F. E. L. Publications (Chicago 1966/1967) p. 4.

10. The Medical Mission Sisters, *Come, Lord Jesus,* Vanguard (1966) No. 7.

11. Charles F. Brown, *Sing 'n' Celebrate* (Waco, Texas, 1971) No. 30.

12. The Medical Mission Sisters, *Joy Is Like the Rain,* Vanguard (1965) No. 9, p. 11.

13. Sister Germaine, *Songs of Salvation,* F. E. L. Publications (Chicago, 1960) p. 9.

14. Stephen Leddy, "Everybody's cryin' out" in *Now,* Hope Publishing (Chicago, 1969) p. 32.

15. James Ooting, "The happening" in *Now,* Hope Publishing (Chicago, 1969) pp. 48-49.

16. Don Wyrtzen, "O give me a soapbox" in *My Soapbox, Folk Songs for the New Generation,* (Rockville Center, N.Y. 1971) pp. 2-3.

17. Sonny Salsbury, "Jesus was just a good guy" in *(More) Folk (Songs) for (Young) Folk,* Sacred Songs (Waco, Texas, 1969) p. 30.

18. Richard K. Avery and Donald S. Marsh, *More, More, More, Hymns Hot and Carols Cool,* Book 2 (1970) p. 16.

19. John E. Walvoord, "We fought a jungle war today" in *Now Sounds,* (Dallas, Texas, 1968) pp. 9-10.

20. Kurt Kaiser, "It's our world" in *Sing 'n' Celebrate,* (Waco, Texas, 1971) p. 38.

21. Sister Germaine, "From among the branches" in *Songs of Salvation,* F. E. L. Publications (Chicago, 1966, 1967) p. 9.

22. "I've got a reason to sing" in *Reason to Sing: A Songbook for Youth Today,* compiled by Norm Shoemaker, Lillenas Publication (Kansas City, 1969) No. 1.

23. Norman Habel, "Christ is changing everything" in *Re-*

sources for Youth Ministry, (1969) Vol. I, No. 3, Hymns for Now II (1969) No. 14.

24. David Collyer, "What people" in Resources for Youth Ministry, (1969), Vol. I, No. 3, Hymns for Now II, (1969) No. 16.

25. M. R. McGervey, "Have you got soul?" in My Soapbox, Folk Songs for the New Generation, (Rockville Center, New York 1971) pp. 60-61.

26. Charles F. Brown, "Reach out and touch" in Sing 'n' Celebrate (Waco, Texas, 1971) No. 29.

27. Peter Scholte, "They'll know we are Christians by our love," F. E. L. Publications, (Chicago, 1966) pp. 2-3.

28. Stephen Leddy, "This is what you're looking for" in Now, Hope Publishing (Chicago, 1969) p. 32.

29. Sister Germaine, "My Lord is long a-comin' " in Songs of Salvation F. E. L. Publications (Chicago, 1966, 1967) p. 30.

30. David Collyer, see note 24.

31. Ed Lyman, "In a silent world" in (More) Folk (Songs) for (Young) Folks (Waco, Texas) p. 17.

32. Peter Scholte, see note 27.

33. "Reach out and touch," see note 26.

34. "Shine" in Sing 'n' Celebrate (Waco, Texas, 1971) No. 50.

35. J. Lorne Peachey, Songs to Be Sung, Whistled, or Hummed (Scottdale, Pa., 1969) p. 5.

36. Dean Kell, Hymns for Now, Workers Quarterly, July 1967, No. 1, Chicago, p. 37.

37. Risk, New Hymns for a New Day, Vol. II, 3 (Geneva, Switzerland, 1966) pp. 21-23.

38. Don Wyrtzen, My Soapbox, Folksongs for the New Generation (Grand Rapids, Mich., 1971) p. 2.

39. Robert Blue, Run, Come See! (Chicago, 1966) p. 1.

40. Ralph Carmichael, He's Everything to Me Plus 53 (Waco, Texas, 1968) p. 3.

41. Charles F. Brown, Sing 'n' Celebrate (Waco, Texas, 1971) p. 82.

42. Ralph Carmichael, He's Everything to Me Plus 103 (Dallas, Texas, 1972) pp. 78-79.

Chapter 10

1. *Studies in Philosophy and Social Studies,* IX (1941) p. 38.
2. Johan Huizinga, *Homo Ludens: (Study of the Play Element in Culture,* (Boston, 1955).
3. Charles Ives, *Essays Before a Sonata,* ed. by Howard Boatwright, (Norton, reprint of 1962 edition), p. 80.
4. John Gensel, "Worship and Jazz," mimeographed notes, p. 7.
5. Quoted in, *Student Musicologists at Minnesota,* V, pp. 177-178.

APPENDIX

A short list of additional readings

Arndt, Elizabeth Rodenbeck. *A Bibliography of Collections of Sacred Folk Music.* Manuscript, 1973.

Carrington, John F. *Talking Drums of Africa.* Westport, Conn.: Negro Universities Press, 1969 reprint.

Courlander, Harold. *Negro Folk Music, USA.* New York: Columbia University Press, 1970.

de Lerma, Dominique-René. *The Black-American Musical Heritage: A Preliminary and Selective Bibliography.* Kent, Ohio: Kent University Press, 1969).
  Black Music in Our Culture. Kent, Ohio: Kent University Press, 1970.
  The Collector's Guide to Recordings of Music by Black Composers. Bloomington, Ind.: Denia Press, 1973.

Fernandez, Fernando Ortiz. *La Africania de la musica folklorica de Cuba.* La Habana, Editora Universitaria, 1965.

Garland, Phyl. *The Sound of Soul.* Chicago: Henry Regnery, 1969.

Kofsky, Frank. *Black Nationalism and the Revolution in Music.* New York: Maerit Book, 1970.

Sargeant, Winthrop. *Jazz, Hot and Hybrid.* New York: E. P. Dutton, 1946.

Schafer, William J. and Johannes Riedel. *The Art of Ragtime.* Baton Rouge: Louisiana State University Press, 1973).

Schuller, Gunther. *The History of Jazz: Vol. 1. Early Jazz: Its Roots and Musical Development.* New York: Oxford University Press, 1968.

Shaw, Arnold. *The World of Soul.* New York: Cowles Book Co., 1970.

Soriano, Alberto. *Tres Rezos Auguricos Y Otros Cantares de Liturgia Negra.* Montevideo: Universidad de la Republica, 1968.

Standifer, James A. and Barbara Reeder. *Source Book of African and Afro-American Materials for Music Educators.* Contemporary Music Project, 1972.

Stearns, Marshall W. *The Story of Jazz.* London: Oxford University Press, 1970.

Wachsmann, Klaus. *Essays on Music and History in Africa.* Evanston, Ill.: Northwestern University Press, 1971.

A short list of recordings

Only these recordings are listed which are mentioned in the text. Many additional recordings and tapes have been listened to by the author.

Missa Bantu. Philipps PCC- 611.

Beaumont, Geoffrey. *20th Century Folk Mass.* Fiesta FLP 25000.

Bernstein, Leonard. *Mass.* Columbia M 231008.

Bianchi, Vicente. *Misa a la Chilena.*

Blue, Robert. *Run, Come See.* F. E. L. S-272.

Brubeck, Dave. *The Light in the Wilderness.* Decca DXS-7202.

Devenish, Bruce, Tom Davidson, Rex Bullen. *A Rock Mass for Love.* Decca D17-5328.

Draesel, Herbert. *Rejoice!* Scepter Records M 10030.

Ellington, Duke. *Concert of Sacred Music.* RCA Victor LSP-3582.

Gere, Frederick H., and Milton H. Williams. *The Winds of God.* St. Paul Episcopal Church, recorded in Grace Cathedral, San Francisco, 94010.

Vince Guiraldi at Grace Cathedral. Fantasy.

Habel, Norman and Richard Koehnecke. *For Mature Adults Only.* Fortress B. 19768.

Lojewski, Harry V. *The Mariachi Mass.* F. E. L. S-382.

Missa Luba, Philipps PCC 206.

Galt MacDermod, *Divine Hair—Mass in F.* RCA LSP-4632.

Mariachi "Hnos Macias" and Jean Larc Leclerc, *Misa Panamericana* Aleluya A-015.

Masters, Joseph. *Missa Brevis.*

Mitchell, Ian Douglas. *The American Folk Song Mass.* F. E. L. CM 6806.

Joe Newman Quintet and John G. Gensel. *O Sing to the Lord a New Song.* Fortress.

Pitts, Clay. *The Mass for Peace.* Avant Garde AVS 116.

Paul Quinlan Trio. *Run Like a Deer Folk-Rock Psalms.* F. E. L. S-092.

Quinones, P. German. *"Misa Incáica" en Quechua.* Lyra LPL-13023.

Ramirez, Ariel. *Misa Criolla*. Philipps PCC-619.

Repp, Ray. *Mass for Young Americans*. F. E. L. S-022.

Repp, Ray. *Second Mass for Young Americans*. F. E. L. S-032.

Ritz, James. *Mass for World Peace*. Tribute TR-106.

Rivers, Clarence Jo. *A Mass Dedicated to the Brotherhood of Man*. Queen's Men Records, Sesac 30.

Toloba, J. and H. E. Lobos. *El Evangelio Criollo*. Music Hall 12-712.

Webber, Andrew Lloyd and Tim Rice. *Jesus Christ Superstar*. Decca DXSA 7206.

Gere, Frederick H. and Milton H. Williams. *The Winds of God*. St. Paul Episcopal Church, in Grace Cathedral, San Francisco, 94010.

44
ԱԲ